5W RETIREMENT BLUEPRINT

LANE G. MARTINSEN

5W Retirement Blueprint

Published 2025 by Lane G. Martinsen
Printed in the United States of America
ISBN: 979-8-9920029-0-4

This publication is designed to provide accurate and authoritative information with regard to the subject matter covered. The information provided is not intended as tax or legal advice and may not be relied on for the purpose of avoiding any individual Federal or State tax penalties. If legal advice or other expert assistance is required, the services of a competent professional should be sought.

Martinsen Wealth Management, LLC is a federally registered investment advisor under the Investment Advisers Act of 1940. Registration as an investment advisor does not imply any level of skill or training. The oral and written communications of an advisor provide you with information about which you determine to hire or retain an advisor. Form ADV Part 2A & 2B can be obtained by visiting https://adviserinfo.sec.gov and search the firm name. Neither the information nor any opinion expressed should be construed as solicitation to buy or sell a security of personalized investment, tax, or legal advice.

Any references to protection benefits or lifetime income generally refer to fixed insurance products, never securities or investment products. Insurance and annuity product guarantees are backed by the financial strength and claims-paying ability of the issuing insurance company.

Edited by Keidi Keating

"You can't go back and change the beginning, but you can start where you are and change the ending."

C.S. Lewis

Retirement planning in the 21st century comes with new challenges as well as new opportunities in our rapidly changing world.

The purpose of this book is to help you think differently regarding retirement income planning, and to help you "unlearn" some of the things you have been taught for decades. The right combination of strategies and good planning can be the difference between a comfortable retirement and financially difficult retirement.

Each chapter builds upon the previous chapter. To get the most out of this book, it is recommended to read each chapter in the normal sequence.

Praise for:
The 5W Retirement Blueprint

Today, as we are living longer, retirement planning is all about income – because savings can run out! This is the number one fear I hear from retirees everywhere. The plan in Lane's book is refreshingly different and more applicable to today's retirement realities. His book shows retirees how to generate lifelong income by making the most efficient use of your total financial picture, a/k/a Holistic Planning. Your money can last as long as you do... and beyond. Consider this book a user's guide to a 21st century retirement plan.

Ed Slott, CPA
Founder of Ed Slott's Elite IRA Advisor Group SM

"This book should be mandatory reading for all of those who are getting serious about retirement or want to confirm they are doing things right while already retired. One of the only books I have found that gives the readers a holistic overview about what financial tools are available to them with a simple explanation of why they may or may not want those tools as a part of their financial plan. This book explains that there is a different way to build your financial plan, so you can retire worry-free."

Jacob Green, Advisor/Financial Planner
Bend, OR

"As a Retirement Planner and Investment Advisor, I have read many books on retirement planning. Most if not all have been very one-sided. I am impressed with the way the author gives an objective view of both sides as to the value of all the products available. This is really a very good book. Everyone nearing or entering retirement will benefit greatly by reading this book. Congratulations!"

Bob Arnold, Advisor/Financial Planner
Superior Income Group, LLC
Dothan, AL

"This book is very interesting and an easy read. It is full of great options for retirement planning. Using the holistic approach to retirement is the way to go."

Tammy E. Lantz, CPA, PC
Cheyenne, WY

"Lane Martinsen does a great job informing the reader of the current issues facing our generation for retirement. The book is well written, easy to follow, and to the point. I will definitely be making changes to my retirement philosophies on the basis of Lane's Holistic Approach."

Brett A. Brudvik,
Attorney Brudvik Law Office, P.C.

"Mr. Martinsen skillfully explains powerful, complex financial and tax concepts in an easy-to-understand manner. I recommend this book to everyone. The tools presented are sophisticated and robust. However, they are presented in a manner that makes for easy reading, adapted to a level that all can appreciate."

Curtis Farnsworth,
CPA Farnsworth Company, PLLC
Chandler, AZ

"Lane Martinsen leaves no stone uncovered as he makes a convincing case for a holistic approach to retirement planning. Spend some time with this book and take to heart its vital message."

David McKnight
Author of *The Power of Zero*

"Bravo! Very well done. The author has written the most balanced book about retirement I have ever seen. That is no small accomplishment. This book will not insult the intelligence of an experienced investor and will not be over the head of a relatively inexperienced person."

Jerry Iacangelo, Financial Planner
Iacangelo Financial Group, LLC
Bridgewater, New Jersey

"Lane gets it! Retirement planning is so much more comprehensive and complicated than what the average retiree can imagine. It involves multiple moving parts and a myriad of strategies. It is not about the one moving part but about how all the parts fit together and work together as one. This is holistic retirement planning and reading Lane's book should be at the top of your priority list."

Carroll Ramer,
President Ramer Retirement Resources
Rochester, MN

"Having been in the industry for many years, I've had the opportunity to read numerous books on the subject. Lane's book stands out for being exceptionally easy to read and digest, packed with valuable insights and practical tips. I highly recommend this book as an excellent resource for anyone looking to grasp complex topics in an accessible and understandable way."

Jeremy Vaught, CFP®, MBA
Tempe, AZ

"For over 20 years, I have worked with many individuals on planning and preparing for retirement. Lane has done an excellent job explaining the quantifiable benefits of a holistic approach over the traditional one-size-fits-all method. If you're looking for an easy-to-understand guide on retirement planning, this book will broaden your perspective, helping you see what to prepare for down the road."

Kenneth Holmes, Financial Planner/Advisor
Tucson, AZ

"Lane Martinsen's highly informative book makes the case that it's not enough to accumulate assets for retirement. You need a holistic retirement income plan to help you figure out how to convert those assets into streams of tax- efficient income. Given the fact that this is a complex endeavor, it is best accomplished with the assistance of a holistic retirement income planner."

Robert Klein
CPA, PFS, CFP®, RICP®, CLTC, MBA, MST
Newport Beach, California

Table of Contents

Foreword xvii
Acknowledgements.. xix
Chapter 1 Financial Advice a la Carte.............. 1
Chapter 2 The Changing Retirement Landscape....................................19
Chapter 3 Achieving a Tax-Free Retirement 33
Chapter 4 Understanding Market Risk............ 53
Chapter 5 Traditional Asset Allocation 70
Chapter 6 The Financial Toolbox 82
Chapter 7 Investments (Red Financial Tools) ... 96
Chapter 8 Annuities and Life Insurance (Green Financial Tools) 125
Chapter 9 Debt, Leverage, and Reverse Mortgages....................................161
Chapter 10 Advisor Alpha and Advisor Gamma...184
Appendix Finding a 21st Century Holistic Retirement Income Planner/Advisor.............................195
About the Author..205

For Tara, our five children, and our growing
circle of grandchildren: This journey,
and all that lies ahead, is for you.

Foreword

By Ed Slott, CPA

Lane Martinsen is back with an all-encompassing plan—a blueprint—to guide you through the 5Ws of managing and preserving your wealth. These are 5 critical areas that everyone seeking financial security in retirement and beyond needs to address. The problem is that most people are overwhelmed by the numbing complexity of it all, when you combine the income, investment, tax, healthcare and estate planning goals you'd like to achieve. It is unfairly confusing, especially when the tax rules keep changing, and the goal posts seem to keep moving. Not to worry—Lane Martinsen once again sorts this all out for you here. He takes you through this maze of information, boils it down, and shows you what to do each step along the way. It's very easy to follow, and you'll be amazed at how much you learn. You'll find the plan that works for you and your family. In addition, the concise summaries of the key concepts at the end of each chapter are invaluable. They help you cement your knowledge and boost your confidence. Dig in and see for yourself!

- Ed Slott, CPA, Retirement Expert
  Founder of www.irahelp.com
  Founder of ***Ed Slott's Elite IRA Advisor Group*** SM

November 15, 2024

Acknowledgements

As I think about what I have learned and experienced over many years, I am simply overcome with gratitude. I have been blessed with so many great mentors in my life and career. I have been able to learn from many of the best and brightest within the financial services industry.

I've felt a need to write this book for several years, but taking the time to actually do it was an overwhelming thought. As one that enjoys setting and achieving goals, I knew I needed to eat the elephant one bite at a time. I made the determination to write at least one chapter, so I could better evaluate a realistic time frame to complete the book. After completing the first chapter, my confidence as a writer began to grow along with my determination to finish the book.

To the dozens of financial professionals, clients, and friends that read my manuscript and served as a sounding board, I give a wholehearted thanks.

A special thanks to my daughter, Mariah Payne for her proof-reading skills and attention to detail. Likewise, to Scott Shaw for his insights and to my assistants, Kelly Gloria, Michelle Garcia, and my talented editor, Keidi Keating.

I extend a heartfelt thanks to the financial advisors who have inspired me along the way, including Kyle O'Dell, Robert Van Sant, Sherry Bohannon, Bob Arnold, Jeremy Shipp, Don Blanton, and David McKnight.

Next, I am grateful to the professors at the University of Arizona and The American College of Financial Services, particularly David Littell and Jamie Hopkins. Also, thanks to Robert Klein, Don Graves, and Wade Pfau for their research and insights.

Furthermore, I wish to thank countless other individuals who have had a profound impact on my life. A partial list must include my brothers, Stewart and Dan, and my sisters, Lynette and LaDawn. Also, Joe Tate, Greg Banks, Richard Baron, Mac Bay,

Shawn McLelland, Rod Pollary, Mark Goaslind, and Tom LaPoint.

Special thanks to Lyle and Lora Martinsen, my dear mom and dad, for their lifetime examples of service to others and for instilling in me an entrepreneurial spirit at a young age. Their love and confidence in me have been a constant strength in my life.

My heart is full of gratitude for my beautiful wife, Tara. None of this would have been possible without her love and support over the past three decades. She is an amazing wife and mother of our five children, Alex, Mariah, Abe, Lora, and Emma.

Chapter 1

Financial Advice a la Carte

"Houston, we have a problem." These were the famous words of astronaut James Lovell, captain of the Apollo 13 space mission in 1970. The astronauts on board were about to join the elite few who had the privilege of landing and walking on the surface of the moon. Two days into their lunar landing journey, their dreams were dashed, and the mission was aborted after the unexpected explosion of one of the oxygen tanks. The damage caused by the blast resulted in a loss of power and cabin heat. The situation turned dire and life-threatening as carbon dioxide levels started to rise.

The mission was not accomplished, and the dream was not realized, because of unexpected problems. The astronauts' very survival was in question, and they did not seem to have enough power to return to Earth. They managed to conserve the remaining power and control the carbon dioxide levels with some makeshift repairs and after seven days in space, they miraculously made it safely through the earth's atmosphere and splashed down in the southern part of the Pacific Ocean.

A variety of potential problems can arise and disrupt any long journey. In the case of Apollo 13, the problems started long before launch day. A flawed design of the oxygen tank's thermostat fan caused an arc between wires that caused combustion in one of the pressurized tanks, which resulted in the devastating midflight explosion.

With the knowledge gained and lessons learned from this perilous voyage, the engineers and rocket scientists made the necessary improvements and preparations for future lunar missions. Apollo 14 was launched in 1971 and successfully landed on the moon as did other manned and unmanned space missions.

You will face many potential problems during your retirement journey that could deplete your financial resources prematurely. Quality planning and preparation can make a tremendous difference in protecting and increasing your retirement income and assets. Before your retirement launch day, be sure your income plan is optimized and achieving "gamma." Gamma is the word used to describe the increase in spendable retirement income. Gamma is achieved through comprehensive holistic retirement planning.

Retirement planning in the 21st century comes with both new challenges and new opportunities in our rapidly changing world.

Retirement is a Modern-Day Concept

Retirement income planning is a relatively new and distinct field within the financial services industry. The idea of retirement is really a modern-day concept. For most of human history, our life expectancy has been less than 50 years of age. In 1900, the United States average life expectancy was only 49 years, and by 1935, the life expectancy had increased to 62 years. The leading causes of death in the past were infectious diseases, such as pneumonia, flu, and tuberculosis. Advancements in modern medicine have been truly remarkable since 1923 when Alexander Fleming discovered the world's first antibiotic.

We are living much longer nowadays, and since about 1970, our time in retirement has grown substantially. This added longevity has put greater demand on our financial resources with increasing health care costs and many other financial needs throughout our extended senior years. At the same time, the financial services industry in general has experienced explosive growth. As a result, there is more financial complexity than there was even a generation ago.

When it comes to retirement income planning, in the 1980s and 1990s, much of the financial advice that was considered "good advice," if given today, would be considered far less than good and even harmful because so much has changed. The problem is many financial advisors and financial companies are still giving the same outdated advice. They are stuck in the past and have not stayed current with the changing times. That may sound like a bold over- statement but keep reading, and I will demonstrate how true it is.

Uncorrelated Financial Planning is the Norm

Holistic financial planning is something most people have never experienced. The financial advice you have typically received is given in an à la carte fashion. For example, at work you may have a 401k, 403b, TSP, or a similar type of employer-sponsored retirement contribution plan. The advice and information you may have received was specific to the amount you should contribute and the options available to you within the plan, but the many other financial aspects of your life are assumed to be separate and unrelated issues.

When you purchased a house and obtained a mortgage, you received financial advice specific to that one transaction. The realtor or loan officer at the bank probably wasn't thinking much about other "unrelated" financial matters that you have or will have in the future; it's simply beyond the scope of what they do.

When you file your taxes each year you may have received some professional advice from a CPA or other tax professionals but again, the advice is generally limited to the task at hand, which is that year's tax return. When you purchased auto insurance, or life insurance, or financed or leased a car, those were separate transactions, and you probably received some advice specific to those events or transactions only.

Uncorrelated and limited financial advice is the norm. YOU are the only connecting link and YOU are the one who must make sure all the financial pieces in your life fit together for your good. We might get by with à la carte financial advice during our working years, but when it comes to retirement income planning, it is a much bigger task. Many parts will make up the whole. Uncorrelated financial advice results in financial inefficiencies and will cost you more than you may realize. Holistic planning can help you leverage unrealized opportunities.

We are experiencing a retirement income planning revolution. The word "revolution" is defined as a fundamental or complete change. The problem is, the majority of us are not aware of the details of what is happening, including many financial advisors who are doing things fundamentally the same way they have been done for decades.

The Purpose of This Book

In this book, I will demonstrate that tremendous financial value can be obtained with intelligent, holistic financial planning. The difference between a typical plan versus a comprehensive holistic plan will translate into more retirement income, long-term portfolio sustainability, and the peace of mind that will come as a result.

As a holistic financial planning practitioner, I can tell you that when the many separate financial elements of your life are holistically coordinated and optimized, financial synergy happens.

Synergy and Advisor Gamma

Within the financial planning industry "Advisor Gamma" is the relatively new term used to describe the synergy that results from holistic planning. The key concept is based on the fact that "the whole is greater than the sum of its parts." More about Advisor Gamma later in the book but, for a conceptual example, when manufacturing a product with four workers, if each person can individually produce five units per hour, you get twenty units per hour in total; but when working together they can create efficiencies, and leverage their individual strengths, together they can produce thirty units per hour. This is synergy. The individuals working together produce more than they could on their own. In a retirement planning context this synergy is referred to as gamma.

You have many separate elements that make up your whole financial situation. When we can holistically coordinate the various parts into one optimized plan, financial synergy happens, which translates into increased wealth, reduced risk, and more cumulative retirement income. Every situation is unique, but the benefits of a good plan can make a lifestyle-changing difference.

Two Sides of Your Financial Mountain

A retirement income plan is necessary to help you meet your financial needs for the rest of your life. **The greatest fear of those heading into retirement, or already in retirement, is the fear of running out of money before they run out of life.**

During the 40 to 45 years of our working careers, we save, invest, and contribute to our retirement accounts with the goal of eventually having our money work for us instead of us working for our money.

From my experience, people often see retirement as "the goal" to achieve. However, as they approach retirement, they realize the real goal is to be able to "stay retired." Your career is like hiking up a large mountain in an attempt to reach the top, which is the retirement goal. But as you get near the top you look down and realize you have a long and dangerous journey to go down the other side of the mountain. To ensure a comfortable retirement, you need to make sure you can get all the way down safely. Will your assets carry you all the way down or will they run out early and leave you stranded midway?

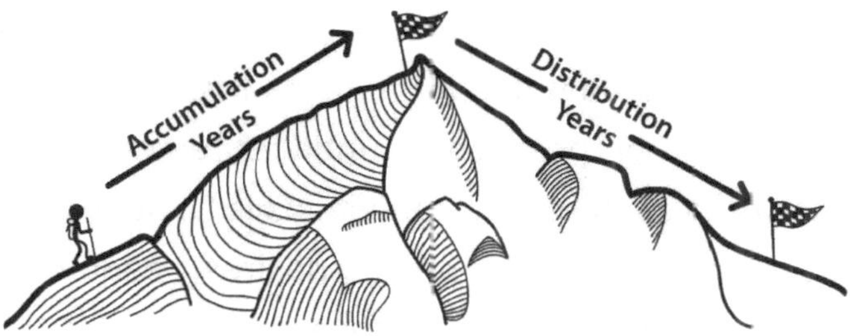

Two sides of your financial mountain: Accumulation side (working and saving years), and the Distribution side (living in retirement).

Will your nest egg sustain you and your spouse (if married) for up to 30 to 35 years of retirement? What might go wrong during three decades of retirement, and how can you best prepare for the journey?

How Much Can You Safely Spend in Retirement?

Pre-retirees approaching retirement ask many of the same questions. How much is too much to spend? Will I run out of money midway through retirement? What are the risks that could cause me to deplete my nest egg prematurely? What is the best order of withdrawal? What types of accounts should I use? How much risk should I assume? What is the best Social Security strategy? What is the best way to manage debt or a mortgage? What about healthcare costs? What about Required Minimum Distributions (RMDs), and what about the taxes that have been "deferred" or postponed until retirement? The answer to each of these questions is "it depends." It depends upon your needs, desires, resources, and many other factors that we will explore in the coming chapters. To find your specific answers requires comprehensive planning.

As people approach retirement, many come to the realization that the financial advisor who may have helped them get to the top of the mountain is not the advisor best qualified to help them create a comprehensive retirement income plan to get them all the way down the other side.

The financial services industry is vast and complex and full of a wide variety of financial service professionals and companies each with their own strengths, weaknesses, and areas of focus. When you have a problem with your foot, it would be wise to consult with a podiatrist. Although a podiatrist is a skilled medical doctor, he or she is not the best choice if you have a heart condition. Likewise, if you need surgery on your foot, a cardiologist is not well qualified for that job. Just as there are many specialties and areas of focus within the medical profession, there are areas of specialization within every profession, including the financial services industry. However, these specializations and qualifications are not as easy to identify.

Most financial advisors spend their time helping people on the accumulation side of the mountain. In contrast, a relatively small number of financial advisors are true holistic retirement income planners. Making good investments and accumulating enough assets during your career is crucial, and there is great value in using a good financial advisor to help you reach your retirement goal. However, how you plan to use those assets and turn them into streams of tax efficient income is a complex financial planning matter and best accomplished with a specialist in retirement income planning.

In retirement, you will still have to deal with many of the same life challenges. Additionally, you have many new challenges and risks that you did not have to deal with during the accumulation years. These include the daunting tax implications of tax deferred retirement accounts, RMDs, sequence risk, longevity risk, increasing health care costs, Social Security taxation, withdrawal sequence, inflation risk, and many others.

Mike and Linda were within one year of retiring. Mike, an engineer, and Linda, a teacher, both had been contributing to their company retirement plans. Mike had a 401k and an IRA and Linda had a 403b plan and a small pension. They had accumulated a nice retirement nest egg but still had about $160,000 remaining on their mortgage. The first time I met with them they said, “We think we have done fairly well with saving for retirement, but we are nervous about the idea of actually withdrawing money for income.” They were hoping to travel and really wanted to purchase a lakeside cabin if possible. They were unsure of what the future tax burden would be. They were confused about Social Security claiming strategies and the best way to manage their investments going forward. When it came to planning for their retirement income (decumulation) for the next 30 years, they realized there were many questions they were unsure about.

Beware of Outdated Financial Advice

Many of the long-time rules-of-thumb are no longer accurate in our rapidly changing world. However, conventional wisdom steeped in outdated financial advice is still overwhelmingly common. When planning your journey down the other side of the mountain, you want to make sure you adequately address each of the potential risks. You can't afford to make mistakes. In Chapter 11 we give you ten specific insights to help you find the right kind of financial planner to help map out a retirement income plan. The following chapters will identify modern-day problems and modern-day solutions within our rapidly changing world that every pre-retiree should understand. Each chapter builds upon the previous chapter. To get the most out of this book, it is recommended to read each chapter in the normal sequence.

A Good Plan Makes a Big Difference

Before an airplane takes flight, a comprehensive written flight plan with all the details is required. The flight plan includes fuel requirements to get from point A to point B. It also includes contingency plans and identifies the locations of every airport between the starting point and the desired destination. The flight plan provides the pilot with information about the aircraft, the number of passengers, the maintenance schedule, and reports. The pilot will not take off before he or she has assessed the weather and wind conditions. Nor will the pilot take off until air traffic control gives authorization and runway clearance.

At any given moment in time there are about one million people in flight around the globe. This vast number has been referred to as the "city in the sky." The complex logistics and planning required to support a million airborne people is impressive to say the least. What's even more impressive is the incredible safety record of commercial air travel. The statistical odds of dying in a commercial flight is around 1 in 11,000,000. In 2017, we had one of the best years ever recorded without a single commercial flight fatality. When you consider the enormous number of miles traveled over the course of a year, it is a truly remarkable accomplishment.

In contrast, the odds of dying in an automobile crash are about 1 in 5,000. The number of fatalities every year is in the tens of thousands, in the United States alone. It's not a true apples-to-apples comparison but my point is that good planning makes a big difference. The odds of success are substantially improved. This is especially true with retirement planning. A holistic and comprehensive retirement plan will greatly increase the likelihood of retirement success.

Uncorrelated Planning Results in Financial Inefficiencies

Before we start our descent down the other side of the mountain, it is critically important that we identify potential risks that we may face during our retirement journey. What could possibly go wrong over the next 30-plus years that could disrupt our plan and deplete our retirement nest egg prematurely? Continuing with the mountain analogy, what if we get bit by a poisonous snake along the way? Or—what if we encounter an intense lightning storm and strong gusts of wind? How will we manage to keep warm and avoid frostbite during a cold winter?

Heading out for a long backpacking excursion in the wilderness can be extremely dangerous if ill-prepared. On the other hand, a well-thought-out plan with all the necessary preparations, equipment, and provisions can make the experience safe, enjoyable, and fun.

Losing Money Unknowingly and Unnecessarily is Common

The typical couple or individual will have many inherent inefficiencies within their financial life. Financial inefficiencies come at a cost and will compound over time, resulting in additional lost opportunity costs. For example, if you lose a dollar unnecessarily to taxes, you lose more than a dollar: You also lose the future dollars that the dollar could have earned for you. Many people are losing and will continue to lose money in various ways, unknowingly and unnecessarily. A good financial plan will identify the inefficiencies, the risks, and the weaknesses, and implement solutions that can make a true difference.

We don't know exactly how long the journey will last or how long we will each live, but we need to plan for as long as we and/or our spouse might live. If you anticipate a life expectancy of age 85 and have a financial plan that will cover you only up to that point you could run into some real problems if you live past that age. Imagine you end up living to 91 years of age instead. From a financial perspective, those last six years could end up being the most difficult of all for you and your family. Of course everyone's situation is unique. A good retirement plan should generally anticipate a minimum of 30 years in retirement.

Because of the long-term nature of retirement planning and the many variables that we may encounter in the years to come, we must evaluate the landscape and attempt to see what's on the horizon as well as what might be just around the corner. We need to be forward-looking and do the best we can to identify the major risks and the potential threats that could deplete our retirement assets prematurely. When we have a good understanding of the major risks we might face, only then can we better prepare and establish safeguards and contingency plans.

Summary:

- Retirement is a modern-day concept.
- We face many risks in retirement that can deplete our assets prematurely.
- Gamma comes from holistic planning and results in more retirement income.
- There are two sides of your financial mountain: Accumulation and Decumulation.
- Do you know how much you can safely spend in retirement?
- Beware of outdated or transactional financial advice.
- A good plan will make a big difference.
- Uncorrelated planning results in financial inefficiencies.
- Losing money unknowingly and unnecessarily is common.
- Great value can be added with comprehensive and holistic planning.

Chapter 2

The Changing Retirement Landscape

Good Planning Requires Vision of the Future

We must start the planning process with a vision for the years ahead. As we evaluate the retirement landscape, we can see both opportunities and challenges on the horizon.

Our country and our entire world have experienced incredible changes during the first two decades of the 21st century. Some changes are easy to see, such as the advances in technology, which have shrunk the world and accelerated the pace of business and everyday life. The political landscape around the world and here at home is continually changing in ways unimagined. Our world is complex with a 24/7 news cycle and information overload. I think back to what life was like growing up in the 1970s and 1980s, and it's amazing to see how much has changed!

Our Financial Environment Continues to Change

Within our financial world many things have changed, and are changing, that may be less visible. Holistic retirement planning has never been as important or as valuable as it is today.

Threats exist that can deplete our retirement assets prematurely. Good preparation is essential. And the first step is to identify and understand the potential problems we may encounter during our retirement years.

Drawing was a team effort by my daughters: Mariah, Lora, and Emma

The Impact of an Aging Population and Shrinking Workforce

The demographics of our population in the United States are rapidly changing. The great Baby-Boomer generation is leaving the workforce at a rate of 10,000 per day. That's about 300,000 every month and 3.6 million every year, and it will continue at that rate until 2030!

The Baby Boom generation began in 1946 as soldiers started returning from WWII, and it continued until 1964, an unprecedented birth rate that lasted for 18 years and represents 75 million Americans. My dad was one of those soldiers and is a WWII veteran. When the war started, he watched his older brothers go off to war. He was eager to serve his country too but had to wait until he was old enough. As soon as he turned 18, he enlisted and served in the US Navy during the tail end of WWII. One of six children, I was born at the very end of the Baby Boom generation in 1964. Had I been born a few months later, I would have been part of Generation X, but I'm a proud member of the Baby Boom generation.

My dad has always had a deep patriotic love for our country and our flag, as do I. No country is perfect.

Yet, despite our weaknesses, I believe we are still, as Abraham Lincoln said, "The best nation ever given to man."

We need to consider the economic impact of an aging population and a shrinking workforce. How might this impact us economically? What might be on the horizon that could potentially disrupt or negatively impact your retirement?

Our Nation's Financial Imbalance is a Big Problem

I had the opportunity to interview the former top CPA of the Federal Government, Mr. David Walker, who was the Comptroller General of the United States and the head of the Government Accountability Office. Mr. Walker went before Congress, prior to his retirement in 2008, to discuss the nation's financial obligations. He used a chart with two lines to demonstrate what will happen as the 75 million Baby Boomers grow older and start leaving the workforce. He presented a chart similar to the illustration below.

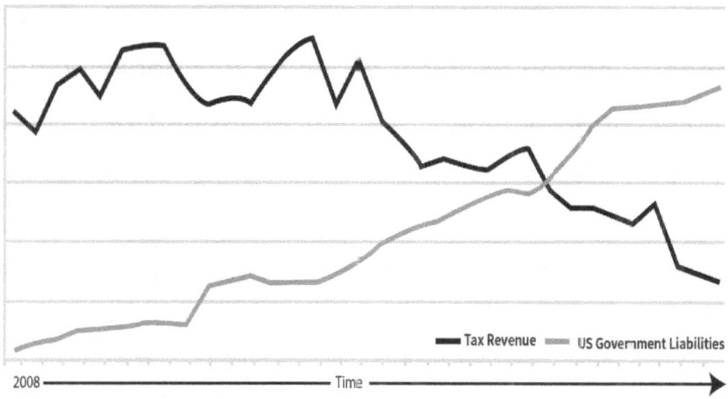

The top line represents tax revenue. Over time, it decreases as our population ages and retires. The bottom line represents the increasing liabilities, which include Social Security, Medicare, Medicaid, government backed pensions, and the growing cost of interest on the national debt.

Our National Debt and Deficits are Mathematically Unsustainable

Mr. Walker boldly stated that we are on an "unsustainable path." He said we can continue to kick the can down the road but there will come a point in time when the two lines will converge, and we will have a major crisis to deal with.

If you have not visited USDebtClock.org I would encourage you to do so. As I write this book, we are rapidly approaching $37 trillion of national debt, and it is growing by nearly two trillion dollars every year. We have never been in this situation. No country in the history of the world has ever been in this situation.

Federal Government 2024	
Tax Revenue	$4,888,000,000,000
Annual Spending	$6,729,000,000,000
Net New Debt	$1,840,000,000,000
Total Debt	$35,000,000,000,000

Numbers Rounded

It's not easy to relate to such large numbers. One billion is difficult enough but when we get into the trillions it is difficult to comprehend exactly how large these numbers are.

To help put this into perspective, it may help if we remove some of the zeros and look at this in a way that we can personally relate. While looking at the illustration below, think in terms of your own personal finances. For this little exercise you need to use your imagination and assume for a minute what it would feel like if the hypothetical scenario below was your own personal scenario.

Hypothetical Personal Scenario	
Annual Salary	$488,800
Annual Spending	$672,900
Net New Debt	$184,000
Total Debt	$3,500,000

Numbers Rounded

What would you do if this was your personal situation? An annual salary of $488,800 is above average income, but you are spending all of it and more. Not to mention, you already have over 3.5 million dollars of debt stacked up, which is also costing you a fortune in interest. A responsible person with average intelligence would stop overspending and work out a manageable plan to pay down the debt. If you could live on say, $100,000, that would free up $388,800 that could be used to pay down the debt, but what if most of your annual spending was fixed and you were not able to make meaningful cuts in spending? What if your spending was not only fixed but increasing rapidly?

What about the cost of interest on the debt? The interest on our national debt five years ago was just over $300 billion per year. That annual cost has rapidly increased and has now surpassed a trillion dollars all by itself. That's tax money spent that buys us nothing! The interest on our national debt is like an aggressive form of financial cancer. Think of the increasing pressure this creates for higher taxes.

Never Before Have We Been in This Situation

As troubling and problematic as our growing national debt is, if you look down near the bottom of the USDebtClock.org web page you will see the number for "Unfunded Liabilities." This is an enormous number over $220 trillion! This number represents the financial obligations and promises of the Federal Government for which there is no funding and no tax revenue. It includes the promises of Social Security, Medicare parts A, B, and D, Federal Employee benefits, and Veteran benefits, as well as our publicly held national debt.

How can the Federal Government honor the overwhelming promises and financial obligations? Mathematically, it just does not work. Either benefits will have to be drastically cut, or taxes drastically raised, or some combination of the two, but our current path, as Mr. Walker said, is "unsustainable."

The Federal Government's top accountant said, *"Regardless of what politicians tell you, any additional accumulations of debt, absent dramatic reductions in the size and role of government, are basically deferred tax increases... unless we begin to get our fiscal house in order.* ***There's simply no other way to handle our ever-mounting debt burdens except by doubling taxes over time."***

The Congressional Budget Office (CBO) has also said that if Social Security, Medicare, and Medicaid go unchanged, our tax rates would need to more than double over time.

It may be hard to imagine our taxes doubling in the future, but it is also hard to imagine any significant reduction in promised government spending. If we look at the history of tax rates, we can see that at times of national crisis, congress has come together and raised taxes to meet urgent needs.

A Brief History of Tax Rates

U.S. Income Tax Marginal Rates 1913-2024

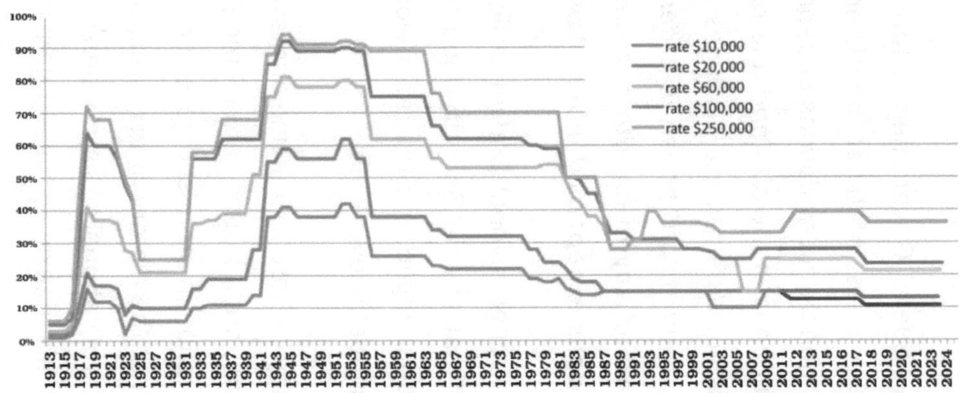

We did not have income tax in our country until 1913 under President Woodrow Wilson. As we entered the WWI crisis, the top tax bracket shot up from 7% to 73%! After the war, the rate came down to 25%. Then, during the great depression, it increased to 63%. At the peak of WWII, the top bracket reached as high as 94%. Over the past 100 years, our top tax bracket has averaged just over 57%. Today our top tax bracket is historically low at 37%.

Some people believe that raising taxes on the rich is a simple solution, but this is not the case. The math does not even come close to providing a solution. Warren Buffett is one of the super-rich in our country. While he happens to think that rich people like him should pay more in taxes as a matter of principle, he also acknowledges that doing so will not solve the problem. There are simply not enough high-income earners to make a meaningful dent in today's debt and deficits.

The poor in our country have nothing to tax and the majority of tax revenue has always come from middle America. I am just touching on the surface of a complex and politically charged subject. There is so much more that could be said about the financial difficulties and complexities we face as a nation. I am not a politician, and this is not a politically motivated book. My role as a financial planner is to help my clients preserve and protect their assets from a variety of potential risks and to navigate the turbulent waters of retirement planning in our ever-changing world.

The point I want to emphasize is that there is a very real risk, and I would say a strong likelihood, that tax rates will be forced higher in the future. So, what does this have to do with retirement planning?

We May Face Higher Taxes in the Future

Most Americans who have done a respectable job of saving for retirement have done so in tax-deferred accounts such as 401ks, IRAs, and pensions.

Another word for tax-deferred is tax-postponed. Postponed until when? Until you start taking distributions in retirement. When we look at our 401k statement or IRA, we tend to think that the balance reflected on the statement is ALL our money, but it is not. The government has a lien on that money!

What percentage of your retirement nest egg will you be able to spend in retirement? Unfortunately, that number is unknown.

Distributions from our tax-deferred retirement accounts will be taxed as "ordinary income." The tax rate will be whatever the income tax rates happen to be in the years we take distributions. We know what tax rates are today, but we do not know what they will be five, ten or fifteen years from now.

This situation creates uncertainty because future tax rates are an unknown variable, subject to change. If we do not know how much of our nest egg we will lose to taxes, we do not know how much money we truly have to work with, which makes creating a long-term retirement income plan difficult.

Taxes are one of our largest expenses and a good retirement plan will minimize or even eliminate our tax exposure in retirement. This huge tax risk problem has been largely underestimated and not even on the radar of most financial firms/advisors, which has put many American's retirement assets at risk.

Summary:

- Good planning requires foresight and anticipation of future events.
- Our world and financial environment continue to change rapidly.

- Do not underestimate the impact of an aging population and a shrinking workforce.
- Our nation's financial imbalance is leading to a major monetary crisis.
- Our national debt and deficits are mathematically unsustainable.
- Never before have we, or any nation, been in this type of situation.
- There is a risk of higher taxes in the future.

Chapter 3

Achieving a Tax-Free Retirement

Rising Taxes: A Major Threat to our Retirement Accounts

It is common for those approaching retirement age to have most of their assets sitting in tax-deferred retirement accounts. This is an example of having received limited-scope financial advice rather than more forward-looking holistic planning. The default advice for decades has been, and still is, to defer taxes whenever possible. This was once sound financial advice, but this is no longer the case. Deferring all taxes until retirement has become outdated advice.

To gain a better understanding, we can categorize nearly all investments into three tax categories. There are a couple of unique exceptions but to keep it simple, I will refer to these categories as tax buckets. Regardless of what types of investments you may have, they will be located in one of the following three tax buckets.

It's important to understand the tax treatment and issues associated with the assets held in each bucket. The first two buckets are the most commonly used and the Tax-Free bucket is greatly underutilized.

The Taxable Bucket (Taxed now)

First, let's start with the Taxable bucket. You might think of it as the "normal tax" bucket because it includes everything that is taxed each year. This includes any type of investment gains you may have in a brokerage account, stocks, bonds, and mutual funds, as well as earned interest in a savings account or CD, dividends, capital gains, and any earned income.

We call this bucket "Taxable" because the realized gains in this bucket are taxed annually. Generally speaking, there is no tax deferral or tax advantage on the gains from assets held within this bucket other than long-term capital gains rates and qualified dividends. If you have investments in this account, each year the IRS is going to tax any realized gains. The 1099s you receive reflect your gains for the year, the amount to be included on your annual tax form.

Out of the three buckets, the Taxable bucket is the absolute worst place to grow money. It is the least tax efficient place to accumulate wealth because the gains are taxed annually.

Taxes Kill the Magic of Compounding

The power and effect of earning compound interest is an amazing thing. Albert Einstein referred to compound interest as the eighth wonder of the world. It has been referred to as the "magic of compounding" and it truly is remarkable. When you attempt to grow wealth in the taxable bucket, the annual tax on the gains simply kills the magic.

To demonstrate, let's look at the effects of compounding with no annual taxes and compare it to an annual tax of 22%. To keep the math simple, I will use the doubling of a penny for 30 days. How much compound growth will you experience?

Doubling of a Penny		
Day	**No Taxes on Gains**	**Gains Taxed at 22%**
1	$0.01	$0.01
2	$0.02	$0.02
3	$0.04	$0.03
4	$0.08	$0.06
5	$0.16	$0.10
6	$0.32	$0.18
7	$0.64	$0.32
8	$1.28	$0.57
9	$2.56	$1.01
10	$5.12	$1.79
11	$10.24	$3.19
12	$20.48	$5.68
13	$40.96	$10.12
14	$81.92	$18.01
15	$163.84	$32.05
16	$327.68	$57.06
17	$655.36	$101.56
18	$1,310.72	$180.78
19	$2,621.44	$321.87
20	$5,242.88	$572.77
21	$10,485.76	$1,019.53
22	$20,971.52	$1,814.76
23	$41,943.04	$3,230.28
24	$83,886.08	$5,749.90
25	$167,772.16	$10,234.82
26	$335,544.32	$18,217.97
27	$671,088.64	$32,427.99
28	$1,342,177.28	$57,721.83
29	$2,684,354.56	$102,744.85
30	**$5,368,709.12**	**$182,885.83**

As you can see, doubling a penny every day for 30 days with no taxes on the gains would grow to over $5.3 million! At this point you are probably wondering how you could get a 100% return every day for 30 days? (Answer: Nowhere.) The point here is not the rate of return, but rather a conceptional side-by-side illustration to compare the impact of being taxed annually on the gains versus not being taxed on the gains. The difference between $5.3 million and $182 thousand is $5.18 million! It's hard to believe that a 22% annual tax can cause that much of a difference.

The Taxable bucket is used a lot because of its simplicity and liquidity. There are no government penalties or restrictions like we have in qualified retirement accounts, but it is not a tax efficient place to achieve compound growth. The Taxable bucket is best used as an emergency fund. An emergency fund should have between three to six months of basic living expenses but any more than a six- month emergency fund, the lost opportunity costs become very expensive over time. Unfortunately, the magic of compounding is not as magical when investments are located in the taxable bucket.

The Tax-Deferred Bucket (Taxed later)

Next let's look at the Tax-Deferred bucket. This is where the majority of Americans have accumulated or are accumulating their retirement nest egg. This would be your employer sponsored plans, such as 401ks, 403bs, TSPs, 457s, and so on. It also includes traditional IRAs, SEP IRAs, and other similar retirement accounts.

It's pretty safe to say that everyone likes a tax deduction. CPAs and other tax professionals are good at finding ways to lower your yearly tax burden, and if that means deferring some of the taxes until future years then so be it. Encouraging tax postponement has been a broadly accepted and common practice for decades and it continues today.

Here are some important things you need to know. Tax preparers and tax preparing software programs focus on saving you taxes in the current year. They will defer, defer, defer as much and for as long as possible because their goal is to help you pay as little in taxes as possible in the short-term, and they do their job; however, you need to understand that they are not planning for many years of retirement. They are not trying to identify the risks that could cause your retirement assets to be depleted prematurely.

The long-time assumption has been that you will be in a lower tax bracket in your retirement years, and therefore it would make sense to postpone as much of the tax burden as possible until then. That may have been good advice in years past but as pointed out in Chapter 2, we face new challenges. The current reality of a shrinking workforce, an aging population, and out of control debt and deficits are at play, and a fiscal crisis is charging at us like a stampede of angry bulls. The likely result of all this will be much higher taxes to come in your retirement years.

Despite the traditional idea that retirees will need less money in retirement, a study* by the Employee Benefit Research Institute (EBRI), found that not to be the case for roughly 46% of retirees. Some expenses in retirement will decrease but new expenses will increase. You may need as much income or more than you had during your working years.

Study*

https://www.ebri.org/health/publications/issue-briefs/content/change-in-household-spending-after-retirement-results-from-a-longitudinal-sample-3291

Distributions from your Tax-Deferred bucket are taxed as "ordinary income" and the tax rate is variable. Your tax burden will be determined by whatever the income tax rates happen to be in the years you take distributions. As mentioned in Chapter 2, you don't know how long your tax-deferred money will last in retirement because you do not know the future tax rates, which are subject to change.

Mathematically Ideal Amount in each Bucket

Now, tax-deferred money is not all bad. Having some money in the Tax-Deferred bucket will typically be good, but only if you have the strategically correct amount. There is a mathematically optimal amount to have in each of the three buckets from a tax efficiency standpoint and getting that right can make an incredible difference in reducing or even eliminating tax risk in retirement. Everyone's situation is unique, so the optimal amount will vary based on your specific situation.

What about tax deductions in the future? Most of the deductions you enjoyed in years past are virtually gone or will be gone in retirement. However, everyone gets a standard deduction. As you take distributions from your tax-deferred accounts in retirement, some of that can come out tax-free based on your standard deduction but having too much in the Tax-Deferred bucket creates tax problems.

The Corrosive Power of Taxes

Qualified retirement plans come with a lot of rules. You cannot take distributions prior to age 59 1/2 without a 10% penalty (there are some exceptions). Additionally, you will be forced to take distributions every year starting on your Required Beginning Date (RBD) whether you want to or not. Previously the RBD was at age 70 ½ but the Secure Act and the Secure Act 2.0 both changed the RBD and now your RBD will vary based on your date of birth. The IRS is well aware that you have not yet paid taxes on your tax-deferred accounts and they are anxiously awaiting the opportunity to start collecting the taxes. If you fail to make the required minimum distributions (RMDs) each year, you will be penalized with a 25% excise tax on the money you were supposed to withdraw but didn't.

For example, if you are required to take a $20,000 distribution for the year and you forget to do it, you will receive a bill from the IRS for $5,000 as well as the ordinary federal and state taxes that are due. So, if your effective tax rate is 25% and you forget to take the required distribution, then you just lost 50% of the money you were required to take out but didn't! Do you think the IRS is serious about collecting the taxes? (Hint: Yes.) They're serious, and there are no senior discounts.

The potential of higher taxes eroding your nest egg in the future is a real threat, and I would argue that higher taxes are unavoidably going to happen. But even if taxes were somehow able to remain historically low throughout your entire retirement, there is yet another very compelling reason to make sure you do not have too much of your nest egg located within the Tax-Deferred bucket. Taxes in retirement are often driven by what I call "tax triggers." These are events or thresholds that increase your tax liability based on your income and Required Minimum Distributions (RMDs). For example, higher income can trigger IRMAA surcharges, increasing your Medicare premiums significantly. Similarly, your total taxable income determines your capital gains tax rate, so larger RMDs can push more of your capital gains into higher tax brackets.

Another tax trigger involves Social Security benefits. A portion of your benefits becomes taxable when your income exceeds certain thresholds (details below). Then there's the widow's tax—a sharp increase in taxes for surviving spouses caused by the change in filing status. Filing as a single taxpayer results in narrower tax brackets and a lower standard deduction, often compounding the impact of other tax triggers.

These tax triggers are often referred to as "stealth taxes" because they quietly increase your tax burden without much warning, leaving many retirees unprepared. Planning ahead can help you mitigate their impact and keep more of your hard-earned money.

Taxes and Social Security Benefits

If your only retirement income is Social Security, then your Social Security benefit will not be taxed. Sadly, this is the case for many Americans. However, if you have a good sum saved in your Tax-Deferred bucket, then it is likely that most of your Social Security benefits will be taxed. Most retirement income plans completely overlook the negative domino effect that occurs when your Social Security benefit gets taxed.

If you look at an IRS 1040 form, you will see in the section titled Income that they want to know how much you received in Social Security income. Next to it, a line for the taxable amount is provided. The IRS formula used to determine if your Social Security benefit will be taxed is referred to as the "Provisional Income" calculation.

The Provisional Income Formula

Provisional income includes any earnings or gains from your Taxable Bucket, which includes other income, e.g., wages, pension, and annuity income. As well as state tax refunds, alimony, business income, rental property income, plus any distributions from your Tax Deferred Bucket, plus 50% of your annual Social Security benefits equals your Provisional Income number.

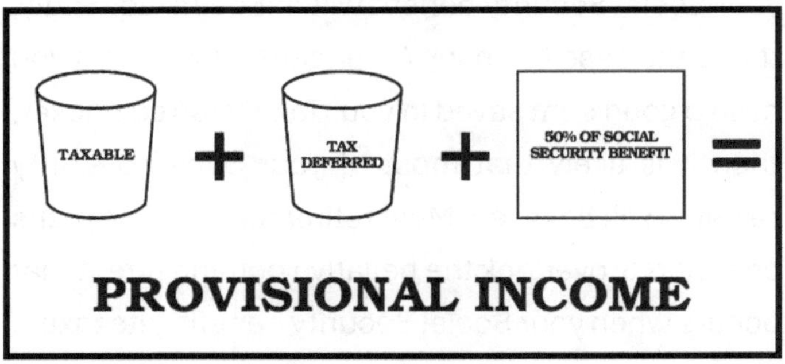

If you are single and your Provisional Income number is greater than $25,000 then 50% of your Social Security benefit will be taxed as ordinary income.

If greater than $34,000, then 85% of your Social Security benefit will be taxed. If you are married the thresholds are $32,000 at 50%, and $44,000 at 85%.

If you have much of a nest egg at all, you will easily surpass the top thresholds, which means most of your Social Security will be taxed as ordinary income and it will be taxed at your top marginal tax bracket. This is a bigger deal than you may initially think. When you have less Social Security income than you had anticipated in retirement due to taxes, to make up for the shortfall, there is a natural tendency to pull more money out of your retirement accounts, which will deplete the accounts more rapidly than anticipated.

When you pull more money out of a tax-deferred account you will need to pull out enough to cover your shortfall plus the additional amount necessary to cover the tax on the additional withdrawal. There is a negative domino effect that has a harmful impact, which is magnified over time.

The good news is that it is possible for most people, depending upon your unique situation, to strategically position your assets such that you can avoid having your Social Security taxed. Doing so will better preserve and enhance your retirement income. Having created many comprehensive retirement plans for my clients, I can tell you that your retirement portfolio will last five to seven years longer on average when you can avoid the Social Security tax. That one strategy alone can make a tremendous difference over time.

Finally, The Tax-Free Bucket (Never taxed)

Now what about this Tax-Free bucket? Is there really such a thing? The more accurate name would be the Tax-Advantaged bucket, but I prefer to call it Tax-Free. The assets held in this bucket can only get in the bucket with after tax dollars, but once the money is in this bucket all the gains are tax free, there are no RMDs, and the money in this bucket is immune to increasing tax rates. We are talking about Roth IRAs, Roth 401ks, Roth 403bs, Roth Conversions, and several other qualified retirement plans preceded by the word ROTH.

The only other non-Roth asset class that can be included in the Tax-Free bucket is strategically structured cash value life insurance. Many people think of municipal bonds as being tax-free, but they are not truly tax-free and do not qualify as part of the Tax-Free bucket.

While the interest earnings from municipal bonds are free from regular federal tax, they are fully counted as part of the provisional income calculation that will cause your Social Security benefit to be taxed. You will still have to pay a capital gains tax if you sell a muni fund at a gain. Also, state tax must be paid on any out of state muni-bond income. So, municipal bonds are not truly tax-free and typically do not accomplish what we need them to accomplish. Another thing to consider is that muni-bonds offer extremely low interest rates and there are often simply better options, which I will get to later in the book.

As of 2024, with a Roth IRA, you can only contribute $7,000 per year if you are under age 50, and only $8,000 if you are over 50. A married couple can each have a Roth IRA for a combined total of $14,000 or $16,000 per year depending upon their age. You must have earned income, and you cannot have too high of an income, or you will be disqualified from contributing into a Roth IRA. However, there are creative but legal ways around the income limit.

Government qualified retirement accounts have a ton of complexity, many rules, and exceptions to these rules. It is not the purpose of this book to break down and identify every qualification, rule, limitation, and penalty for each of these various government qualified plans. There are other books that do that, and they are especially useful when you are having a hard time falling asleep.

The purpose of this book is to help you think differently regarding retirement planning and to help you "unlearn" some of the things you have been taught for decades. The right combination of strategies and good planning can be the difference between a comfortable retirement and financially difficult retirement.

In addition to Roth IRAs, many other retirement plans may have a Roth option. Most 401k, 403b, TSP, or 457b plans do have Roth features, but they are underutilized. The default is often tax-deferred contributions. If so, you need to request that your contributions be designated as Roth rather than traditional. If you do this, keep in mind that if you are getting an employer match, the match will typically go into the traditional tax-deferred account, but all your own contributions can go into the Roth account.

Historically Low Tax Rates Provide a Window of Opportunity

If you are rapidly approaching retirement and you have already accumulated your nest egg primarily in tax-deferred accounts, then you may want to consider Roth Conversions to get the right amount of money shifted into the Tax-Free bucket. The problem is, if you convert all of it in one year it will all be taxed as ordinary income and it will bump you up into the higher tax brackets. The goal is to lower your tax burden, not increase it. You do not want to convert it all at once, but rather, it should be done carefully over multiple years.

Remember, the IRS has a lien on your tax-deferred money and you will be paying taxes on that money. It is as certain as the sun rising in the morning. It's going to happen, so if you owe taxes, would you prefer to pay them at historically low rates or wait until taxes are higher in the future?

What that means is, we have a window of opportunity to get as much of our money shifted via Roth Conversions as we can reasonably accomplish. It requires a multi-year strategy to determine the best amount to convert based on several different factors within your specific situation.

Multi-year Roth Conversion Strategy

Most people who keep their tax-deferred retirement accounts for the long haul will pay a lot of unnecessary taxes. This is because all interest or investment growth is taxed at ordinary income rates, resulting in taxes compounding upon taxes year after year. The table below is a hypothetical comparison of the total potential tax consequences of keeping your tax-deferred account versus implementing a Roth conversion strategy.

Tax-Deferred Account Balance = $750,000		Converted to Tax-Free (over 5 years)	
Total Taxes PAID	$724,493	Total Taxes PAID	$187,500

As you can see, there is a massive difference and significant tax savings with a multi-year conversion strategy. What are the assumptions in this comparison?

- Tax-deferred account balance of $750,000
- Keeping your tax-deferred account from age 64 to an assumed age of 90
- Assumed annual rate of return = 6%

- Assumed tax liability of 25%, including federal and state taxes
- Assumes taxes don't increase but remain the same in all years
- Conversion time period = 5 years

Even assuming taxes don't increase, the advantages of a conversion strategy are still significant. If taxes do increase as we anticipate, the tax liability versus savings will be even more dramatic.

It is important to keep some key concepts in mind before we change subjects. Your money within the tax-free bucket is isolated and protected from future taxes. Distributions from the tax-free bucket do not activate tax triggers or increase your taxable income. They also don't count toward your provisional income, so they won't cause your Social Security benefits to be taxed. Once your money is in the tax-free bucket, it remains truly tax-free forever. Even if tax rates double in the future, two times zero is still zero.

A truly tax-free retirement can be achieved for most people with true holistic planning. Some things such as a pension or rental income may prevent you from achieving a completely tax- free retirement.

There are many variables and factors to consider in mapping out an optimal plan. For now, it's on to another topic, but we will return to this concept shortly.

Summary:

- Rising taxes are a major threat to our retirement accounts.
- Taxes kill the magic of compounding in the taxable bucket (taxed now).
- Locating too much money in the tax-deferred bucket (taxed later) is a problem.
- There is a mathematically ideal amount that should be located in each bucket.
- Taxes have a corrosive power on your assets.
- Social Security benefits will be taxed without proper planning.
- The provisional income formula determines taxes on your Social Security income.
- The tax-free bucket (never taxed) is greatly underutilized.
- Historically low tax rates provide a window of opportunity to reposition assets.

Chapter 4

Understanding Market Risk

My staff and I evaluate and analyze investment portfolios on a regular basis. What I can tell you is that the majority of portfolios that come across my desk have more risk than the client is generally aware of and more risk than they are comfortable with. In other words, it is common for the risk level to be out of alignment with the client's true risk tolerance.

It is important to consider how much risk you really have in your portfolio. How much of your nest egg can you afford to lose in the next market downturn? Will you have the time required to recover from a heavy loss? Losing a chunk of your nest egg in a market downturn can be especially devastating to those near retirement or already retired. Market risk and volatility are dangers that deserve special attention.

Diversification Does Not Protect You from Systemic Market Risk

There are two types of investment risks: those that can be diversified, and those that cannot. All advisors will emphasize the importance of diversification within an investment portfolio (or at least they should). However, being well diversified can also give you a false sense of security. It is important to understand what diversification can and cannot do for you.

Non-Systemic Market Risk (Diversifiable)

The first risk is "specific risk," also called "non-systemic risk." This is the risk associated with specific investments, specific stocks, or specific companies.

Investing in only a few of your favorite stocks is very risky. There are many unexpected things that can cause any company's stock to lose value unexpectedly. Increased competition, mismanagement, and countless other potential problems could develop.

There are many examples of companies holding the promise of a great investment opportunity, only to fall victim to change, economies, or internal turmoil. One example you may remember was Enron. Enron was an energy company based out of Houston, Texas. Before its fall, Enron was the seventh largest company in the United States with a market capitalization of $70 billion. Enron's shares dropped from $90 per share to $0 within a very short period. Corruption and fraudulent accounting led to the company's demise.

If all your eggs were in the Enron basket, your entire nest egg was wiped out. Completely gone!

Another example of specific risk is Blockbuster Video.

Blockbuster had 9,000 retail locations around every street corner in the United States. They dominated the home video market. Then, innovative competition and innovative technology changed everything. When Netflix came along and took over, Blockbuster filed for bankruptcy, and their stock fell to zero.

When you diversify, you spread the risk over multiple companies, and you can avoid the risk of having your entire nest egg depleted from one bad stock. When one company's stock drops, it will have minimal impact on your overall portfolio.

In the two examples above, when the stocks of Enron and Blockbuster lost their value, it was non-systemic to the overall market. This leads us to the second type of risk: systemic risk.

Systemic Market Risk (Non-Diversifiable)

Systemic risk is the risk inherent to the entire market or market segment. It is non-diversifiable market risk. This type of risk is unpredictable and can be triggered by a host of macro-economic possibilities, such as wars, inflation, recessions, market bubbles, and anything that causes instability or fear in the world economy.

The dot-com bubble in the year 2000 triggered a systemic drop in the overall market. The terror attacks just one year later, September 11, 2001, caused the markets to sink further. I remember that time as if it were yesterday. Immediately following the attacks, all the flights were grounded as air travel came to a halt. I had previously scheduled a flight from Salt Lake City to Atlanta, Georgia, which was set to depart just four days after the attacks. I was surprised that my flight did not get cancelled. In fact, it ended up being one of the first flights back in the air.

The flight had many empty seats; most of the passengers had been stranded and were just trying to get back home. I think I was one of the few on the plane who was on a regular business trip. Everyone was on edge, and I remember hearing the emotion in our pilot's voice as he assured us before takeoff that we were going to be safe during our flight. It was a very sobering time for our country.

After two years of market declines, the market started to rebound in 2003 and continued to improve until the later part of 2007, when the subprime mortgage crisis triggered a major market crash. This was the beginning of the great recession. Millions of people lost their homes, their jobs, and a large portion of their investments. The not so funny joke at the time was "my 401k is now a 201k" because their 401k had lost half its value.

After many years of a bull market, people tend to forget that markets are cyclical in nature. Looking back over a 127-year stretch, starting at 1896, we can see that there were five major bull markets and four major bear markets within that time frame. Both bearish and bullish cycles have been for extended periods of time. There are periods of bull market growth and bear market losses.

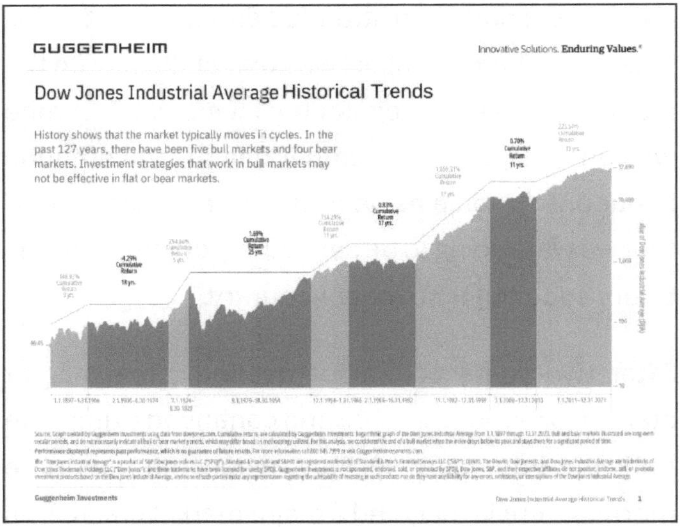

Reprinted with permission from Guggenheim Investments

Source: Graph created by Guggenheim Investments using data from DowJones.com. Cumulative returns are calculated by Guggenheim Investments. Logarithmic graph of the Dow Jones Industrial Average from 1.1897 through 12.2017. Bull and bear markets illustrated are long-term secular periods, and do not necessarily indicate all bull or bear market periods, which may differ based on methodology utilized. For this analysis, we considered the end of a bull market when the index drops below its peak and stays there for a significant period. Performance displayed represents past performance, which is no guarantee of future results. For more information visit GuggenheimInvestments.com. The "Dow Jones Industrial Average" is a product of S&P Dow Jones Indices LLC ("SPDJI"). Standard &

Poor's® and S&P® are registered trademarks of Standard & Poor's Financial Services LLC ("S&P"); DJIA®, The Dow®, Dow Jones®, and Dow Jones Industrial Average are trademarks of Dow Jones Trademark Holdings LLC ("Dow Jones"); and these trademarks have been licensed for use by SPDJI. Guggenheim Investments is not sponsored, endorsed, sold, or promoted by SPDJI, Dow Jones, S&P, and their respective affiliates do not sponsor, endorse, sell, or promote investment products based on the Dow Jones Industrial Average, and none of such parties make any representation regarding the advisability of investing in such products nor do they have any liability for any errors, omissions, or interruptions of the Dow Jones Industrial Average.

The Lost Decade

The total decline in the S&P 500 Price Index from 2000- 2002 was 49.15%, and 2007-2009 was a whopping 56.78%. These events are examples of overall market risk or systemic risk. Regardless of how well you may have been diversified, if you were invested in stocks and bonds, you lost a lot of money. When the markets are good and growing, we tend to forget how quickly things can reverse directions.

Recovering From Losses Can be Difficult

The impact of market losses is often underestimated in regard to retirement distribution planning and is important to understand.

To keep the math simple, let's say you have $100,000 invested in the market. If we experience a 40% systemic market drop, you now have only $60,000.

Scenario 1: What if the market rebounds the following year with 40% growth?

You lost 40% followed by a 40% gain—are we back to where we started?

No. A 40% gain on $60,000 is only $84,000. You are still down 16%.

$100,000	
40% Loss:	$60,000
40% Gain:	$84,000
Total Value Down (16%)	

Scenario 2: What if the market rebounds the following year with 60% growth?

You lost 40% followed by a 60% gain. Are we back to where we started? No. A 60% gain on $60,000 is only $96,000. You are still down 4%.

$100,000	
40% Loss:	$60,000
40% Gain:	$84,000
Total Value Down (16%)	

To fully recover from a 40% loss, it would require a 67% gain to get us back to our original $100,000.

$100,000	
40% Loss:	$60,000
67% Gain:	$100,000
Total Value Down (0%)	

How much time might it take to realize a 67% return? If we assume a 7% growth rate each year, it would take almost nine years! And that is just to get back to where you were before the drop.

> *"The first rule of investing is never lose money. The second rule is never forget rule number one."*
>
> \- Warren Buffett

Recovering from volatile market losses is difficult because you have less money working for you. This is referred to as negative compounding. While compounding can be very positive and work magic on investment growth, it also has a dark side. Negative compounding brought about by market losses has an opposite and detrimental effect. It is more important to "not lose money" than it is to chase the highest gains possible by taking on more risk and the volatility that comes with it.

Volatility is Your Largest Investment Cost

The biggest expense you have when it comes to market investments is volatility. Volatility is not commonly thought of in terms of being a cost of investing, but it really is your largest investment cost. Understanding how to manage and reduce volatility is especially critical for those nearing retirement or in the early years of retirement.

Which sounds better, an average rate of return of 7.5% or 10%? Of course the 10% sounds better, right? In the illustration below, we compare the returns of Option #A and Option #B.

Option #A has some volatility but averages a return of 10% over three years. Option #B has no volatility and averages 7.5%.

Investment (100k Initial Investment)	Year 1	Year 2	Year 3	Average Return	Actual Growth
Option A Returns	+ 30%	- 30%	+ 30%	10%	$118,300.00
Option B Returns	+ 7.5%	+ 7.5%	+ 7.5%	7.5%	$124,230.00

As you can see, average rates of return can be misleading when you forget to factor in volatility. When looking at the actual growth, we can see that the 7.5% average return *without* volatility was clearly a better investment than the 10% average return *with* volatility. It is important to not get lost in return rates alone, but rather focus on the entire equation to bring about the greatest actual growth.

Let's look at another example. The chart below compares the growth of $100,000 with an average rate of return of 10% over five years.

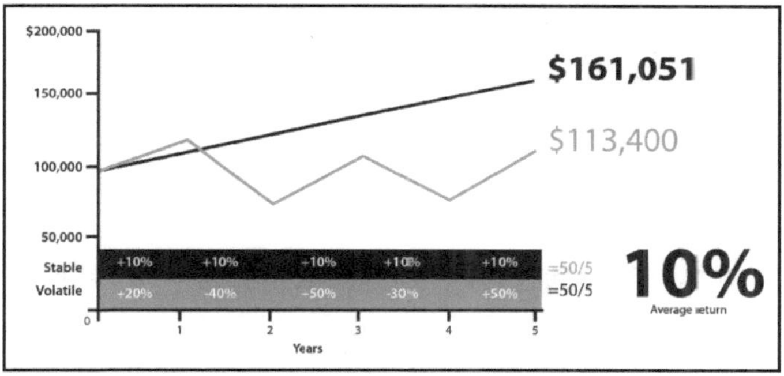

Based on initial investment of $100,000 with earnings compounded annually. Assumes no taxes, fees or other costs of investing. This is a hypothetical example, not an investment in any security.

As you can see, the **Stable** return and the **Volatile** return both averaged 10% growth over five years; however, the investment with no volatility performed substantially better than the investment with volatility. To reiterate again, volatility is the greatest investment cost you will have.

Negative Sequence of Returns

Another important concept to understand when you are approaching your retirement years is the effect of a negative sequence of returns which can cause you to run out of money prematurely.

During your accumulation years, the sequence of market returns from year to year has no impact on your total accumulated amount. Sequence risk is something never experienced during your accumulation years. It only becomes a risk when you are nearing retirement and when you start taking withdrawals from your nest egg in retirement.

As illustrated above, recovering from a market loss is difficult and can take years. If you experience negative returns while you are also taking distributions for retirement income, your ability to recover from losses becomes much more difficult and maybe even impossible.

To demonstrate, let us compare two couples: The Bradys and the Coopers.

Both the Bradys and the Coopers have a nest egg of $500,000 for retirement.

Both couples have the same retirement and income plans. Both couples are using an inflation rate of 3%, both are going to withdraw 5% of their nest egg each year for income. Both have the same investments and they both earn an average rate of return of 9%. Both get the same market returns over a 30-year period, but with one difference, and that is the order of the returns.

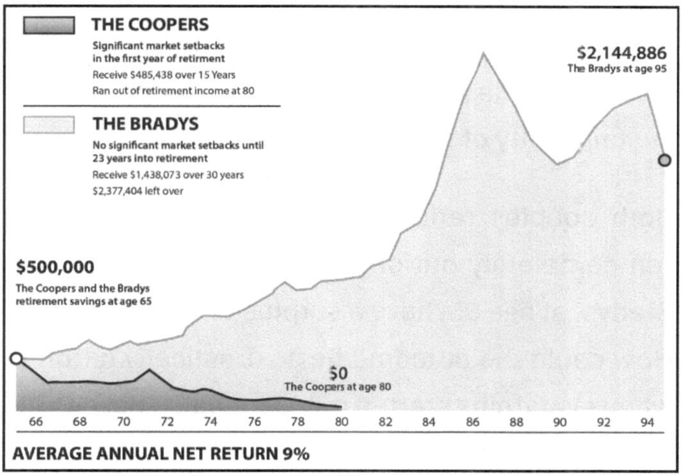

This is a hypothetical example used for illustrative purposes only, assuming an initial premium of $500,000. Chart assumes a 5% rate of withdrawal beginning in year 1, with a 3% annual increase of the net withdrawal amount to account for inflation. Actual S&P 500® historical data from 01/02/1979 to 01/02/2009 has been used in this graph. The hypothetical illustration does not consider the impact of taxes, which would reduce all values. Time period selected because of the extreme volatility during the 2000's, to better illustrate the impact of significant losses early in retirement. Using the current time period would demonstrate less dramatic results. Returns are based upon the Standard & Poor's 500 Index (S&P 500 Index) historical data from 1979-2009. S&P 500 Index returns for the Coopers are in reverse chronological order. The S&P 500 Index is an unmanaged group of large company stocks. It is not possible to invest directly in an index. Past performance does not guarantee future results.

Although both couples experience the same average rate of market returns (9% over 30 years) and both couples experience negative returns, the Coopers experience negative returns in the early years, while the Bradys do not experience them until later in their retirement years. The Coopers' experience with negative returns early on results in their inability to recover and has a profound negative impact on the sustainability of their retirement portfolio.

Both couples retire at age 65 and the Coopers run completely out of money at age 80 while the Bradys, at age 95, have a surplus of over $2 million! How could the outcome be so drastically different when everything started out identical? Answer: The sequence of the returns.

The Bradys were lucky, and the Coopers were unlucky. Luck would have been on your side if you had found yourself retiring in 1990 because the 90s experienced a strong bull market. On the other hand, what if you had retired in 2000? You would have been very unlucky. It took the market ten years to recover from the volatile decade of the 2000s. If you were making withdrawals throughout that decade, you may not have recovered in ten years, if ever. As you can see, experiencing a big market loss at the wrong time in retirement can be devastating.

The Negative Sequence Danger Zone

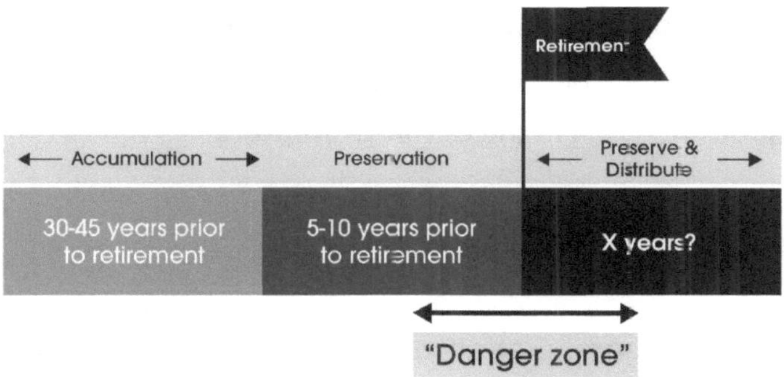

There is something called a negative sequence danger zone: the 15-year window that spans from the five years before retirement until after the first ten years in retirement. Sequence risk becomes most dangerous during that time frame.

The Volatility Buffer Strategy

There are creative ways to better protect your assets from sequence risk, and one of these strategies is to implement a volatility buffer. A volatility buffer is a strategy that requires a combination of both market-based investments and non-market-based assets. The basic concept is to refrain from taking withdrawals from your market-based investments when the market is down, and instead, take withdrawals from other non-market-based assets. This strategy is remarkably effective in reducing the danger of a negative sequence. We will be exploring this and other ways to reduce market risk and sequence risk in the coming chapters.

Summary of Key Concepts:

- Diversification does not protect you from systemic market risk.
- Non-systemic or specific market risk is diversifiable.
- Systemic market risk is not diversifiable.
- The 2000s is referred to as the lost decade.
- Recovering from market losses can be difficult.
- Market volatility is your largest investment cost.
- Negative sequence of returns can deplete your assets prematurely.

- The negative sequence danger zone is a 15-year window of time.
- Using a volatility buffer can substantially reduce sequence risk.

Chapter 5

Traditional Asset Allocation

Outliving your wealth is the number one fear of those heading into retirement. Looking for a job at age 75 or 80 is not on anyone's bucket list. Retirees at an advanced age are not keen on the idea of re- entering the workforce. This may, however, become a reality for some, and it's not likely that they would earn the same income as they had before retirement.

So, how much can you spend in retirement without the fear of running short? Can you really convert your retirement nest egg into sustainable income for the rest of your life, and if married, the life of your spouse? These are major questions for nearly everyone heading into retirement.

The Modern Portfolio Theory

The Modern Portfolio Theory was pioneered by Harry Markowitz and first published back in 1952. The theory is based on the idea that an investment portfolio's risk and return should not be viewed separately. In other words, if you want a higher return then you need to assume more risk. If you want less risk, you need to be okay with a lower return.

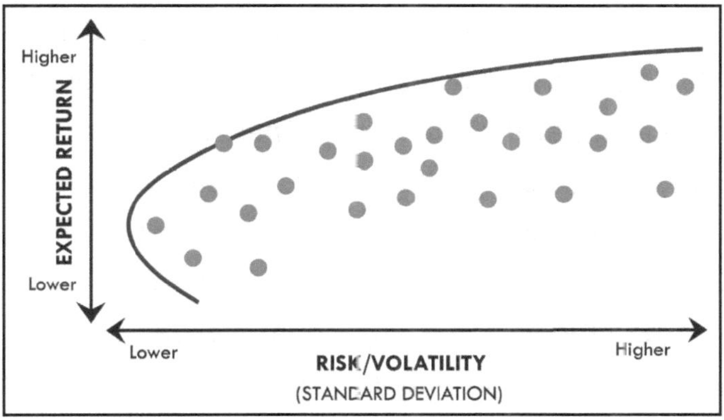

The method for adjusting the risk level within a portfolio is traditionally based on the allocation of stocks and bonds. The theory was broadly adopted, and it remains the prevailing concept of portfolio construction today. The industry term that emerged from the Modern Portfolio Theory is "Asset Allocation." I prefer to call it "Traditional Asset

Allocation" to distinguish it from newer and more stable portfolio allocation strategies, which we will be exploring.

The Safe Withdrawal Rate

When using traditional asset allocation, how much can we withdraw for income each year without depleting our nest egg too quickly?

The 4% rule is a guideline that originated from the research of William Bengen in an article he published in the *Journal of Financial Planning* in 1994. The rule was considered the "safe withdrawal rate." It was broadly adopted by financial advisors, however, there are some major problems with the 4% rule today. The assumptions Bengen used are completely out-of-date in today's world. There has been a lot of new research conducted by many experts and scholars. While their conclusions have differences, nearly all agree that the 4% rule is no longer considered safe.

Why was it considered to be safe in the 1990s and today it's considered risky? What has changed? Two of the key factors are the change in interest rates and in our increasing longevity.

Bengen assumes a traditional asset allocation of 50% bonds and 50% stocks. The income generated from bonds is nowhere near what it was back then. As a result, traditional asset allocation will not perform over time the way it once did, and a portfolio is much more likely to be depleted early when using the 4% rule today.

Bonds: A False Sense of Security

Bonds are generally thought of as the lower risk portion of an investment portfolio and using them reduces volatility and provides less risk to your portfolio mix. Bonds are an essential component of the traditional asset allocation model. Stocks and bonds have different characteristics and while they do have some correlation to each other, the correlation is considered to be low. Bonds will not produce the returns that you can get from stocks over time; however, an all-stock portfolio would be too risky, especially for those just heading into retirement.

A well-diversified portfolio with a mix of asset classes is fundamental to the traditional asset allocation model, but it can give a false sense of security. Bonds have many of their own inherent risks, which include interest rate risk, default risk, reinvestment risk, inflation risk, liquidity risk, and credit downgrade risk. I won't be diving into the details of each of these bond-related risks in this book, however I do feel the need to mention a few key points.

There is an inverse relationship between the price of bonds and interest rates. When interest rates go up, the value of bonds go down. When rates decrease, the value of bonds goes up. If you need to liquidate a portion of your low interest bonds in a rising interest rate environment, you will be forced to sell them at a discount.

The 35-Year Bond Bull Market Has Ended

It is important to understand that for more than 30 years we were in a bond bull market. Interest rates reached their high point in the 1980s and then slowly and steadily decreased for more than three decades. During the recession following the 2008 market crash, interest rates dropped to historic lows and remained low for a prolonged period. The U.S. 10-year treasury yield reached an abnormal low of 1.35% in 2016 and started to increase again in 2018. The long-time bond bull market had officially ended!

With increased inflation and the commencement of a bond bear market, the low yield from bonds today cannot adequately support a 4% withdrawal rate.

Monte Carlo Simulations

In attempting to predict a "safe withdrawal rate," Monte Carlo simulations are used. These simulations (or forecasting model) got their name from Monaco, Monte Carlo, known for its casinos and gambling. The simulations are used to model probabilities with many variables and attempt to estimate chance and random outcomes.

Some Monte Carlo studies say the new safe withdrawal rate is 3%. Other studies say 3.4% or less is necessary to protect against our increased longevity. In any case, there is little dispute that when using the Traditional Asset Allocation model, the 4% rule is no longer considered a safe withdrawal rate and could lead to running out of money prematurely.

Unpredictable Retirement Income

A new trend among some advisors is to recommend a flexible 4% rule. Meaning, if you are flexible with your income level from year to year, and you are okay to reduce your income based on market performance, then you may be able to make it work without depleting your portfolio completely. While this may work for some, an unpredictable income makes planning difficult and does not provide the peace of mind most hope for in retirement.

Life Expectancy Nearly Doubled During the 20th Century

Another contributing factor to the 4% rule failure is the fact that we are living longer and need our portfolio to provide income for longer periods of time.

When looking at life expectancy numbers, it is important to know that the numbers used are averages from birth to death and don't give an accurate picture for the Baby Boomer generation heading into retirement. We have many social ills taking the lives of Americans at an alarming rate, such as the opioid drug epidemic and increased suicide. Tobacco users and the many people who live generally unhealthy lifestyles all contribute to the life expectancy national average of 79 years of age. It is important to keep in mind, however, if you are in generally good health at age 65 today, then your life expectancy is much longer than the overall national average.

A 65-year-old couple today has a 25% chance that one partner will live to age 97, and a 50% chance that at least one of the partners will live to age 93.

My mom and dad are a classic example of increased longevity. They were married for over 66 years before my dad passed away. He lived to almost 94, and my mom, currently well into her 90s, still works in her garden, has an active social life, and lives independently. What makes it more amazing is that 30 years before my dad's passing, at age 64, he had open-heart bypass surgery. He also had other health issues that were resolved with quality modern-day health care. If my dad had been born just one generation earlier, the sophistication of health care would not have been available, and his life would no doubt have been much shorter.

As I pointed out in Chapter 2, we have an aging population. Many times, when I am speaking in front of a large group or teaching a retirement planning class, I ask if they have an idea of which segment of our population is the fastest growing segment, and most people guess age 65, but the fastest growing segment of the US population are those aged 85 and older.

Back in 1950, in the United States, there were approximately 3,000 centenarians who had reached age 100 or more. By 2050, the number of centurions will reach 1 million in the United States alone! Think about that for a moment, one million Americans over age 100. Even more astounding, by 2050, the worldwide number of centurions is projected to be 4 million.

Longevity is a Risk Multiplier

While living longer is almost unarguably a good thing, longevity is a risk multiplier when it comes to financial planning. More time in retirement means there is more time for all the other possible risks to become a problem for you.

Increased life expectancies increase the chance that you or your spouse may need long-term care in later years. We are at risk of chronic illness, injury, disability, and the effects of the aging process, including cognitive impairment, such as Alzheimer's disease.

Everyone hopes to remain independent throughout their life, but according to the U.S. Department of Health and Human Services, the reality is that about 70% of us will need some form of long-term care and about 40% of us will need care in a full-time nursing home for some period of time. These things combined, it is imperative to consider the need for long-term care as part of a holistic retirement plan.

Long-Term Care

The topic and details of long-term care insurance and the possible alternative options deserves its own separate book.

I will only touch on this subject lightly here and highlight some key points to keep in mind.

The median cost for long-term care in the United States is $285 a day or $8,669 per month for a semi-private room in a nursing home. Alternatively, a private room will run you $320 a day or $9,733 per month on average.

Your retirement nest egg could be wiped out by a long-term care event and impact the healthier spouse within a marriage. This could result in your loved one being left in a very difficult financial position for many years.

Relying on family members or friends to provide care could likely become a regrettable decision. Even if a family member is willing and has the right training, they can become overwhelmed by the stress and time commitment of managing their own life and family on top of providing on-going care for an aging parent.

Long-term care insurance is anything but cheap and has become increasingly difficult to qualify for. This is especially true if you have any health issues, or even if you have a family history of dementia or Alzheimer's.

Medicare does not cover long-term care expenses. Medicaid does, but you will not qualify for Medicaid if you or your spouse have some assets. Medicaid is a low- income program and it requires you to spend down your own household assets first before you can qualify. There are some new innovative ways to address the long-term care risk, which will be explored in Chapter 9.

Using a traditional asset allocation investment portfolio exclusively will provide less income than in years past. It is outdated and too risky for most retirees. There are some excellent alternatives to bonds that we will be exploring in Chapter 8.

Summary:

- Traditional asset allocation has more risk than newer allocation strategies.
- The safe withdrawal rate of 4% is no longer considered to be safe.
- The new safe withdrawal rate when using traditional asset allocation is closer to 3%.
- Bonds provide a false sense of security.
- The 35-year bond bull market has ended.
- Monte Carlo simulations estimate random outcomes with a wide range of outcomes.
- A flexible withdrawal rate creates unpredictable retirement income from year to year.
- Longevity is a risk multiplier because you need more money for more time.
- Long-term care planning should not be overlooked.

Chapter 6

The Financial Toolbox

The Need for Financial Institutions

Is it possible to effectively manage our money without the use of financial institutions and financial products? The answer is no. Whether we like it or not, we need the benefits that financial institutions can provide through their products and services.

Financial products are provided by a variety of financial institutions, such as banks, credit unions, brokerage firms, asset management firms, custodians, mutual fund companies, various insurance companies, mortgage bankers, and government sponsored entities.

If we wanted to avoid using financial products altogether and instead stash our cash under the mattress, we would open ourselves up to many new risks and lost opportunity costs. A long-term all cash position would be costly, risky, and unwise.

The Impact of Inflation

Cash loses its buying power over time because of inflation. From 1917 to 2017 inflation has averaged 3.24% per year.

What one dollar can buy today is much less than what it could buy in years past.

How much did your parents pay for their first house? How much would that same house sell for today? The difference in those numbers demonstrates the impact of inflation. To maintain its buying power, your money cannot sit idle, but rather, it needs to grow at the rate of inflation at the very least. This simply cannot be accomplished with all cash. The solution is to use financial instruments wisely and strategically.

If not under the mattress, then where should we put our money? There is a plethora of financial products and countless ways to invest and hold our assets. So, what's on the financial menu and how do you best choose where and how to position your assets?

Attributes of the Perfect Investment

For just a minute, I want you to imagine there is such a thing as a perfect investment. What attributes would the perfect investment product have?

Attributes of The Perfect Investment	
– High rate of return – No market risk – Tax deduction on contributions – Tax-free growth – Tax-free distributions	– 100% liquidity use and control – No fees – No penalties – Guaranteed income stream for life – Guaranteed to pass to heirs tax-free

This would unarguably be an incredible investment product, but does it exist? Unfortunately, it does not. However, all the attributes listed above do exist and can be found within the full menu of financial products. They just don't exist all together within any one financial product.

The Right Combination of Financial Products

A good retirement plan should be customized to your individual situation. It will often include a mix of financial products, depending upon their unique strengths and attributes to achieve an optimal result.

It is helpful to think of financial products, financial institutions, and investments as financial tools. We use tools to build and fix things, and we want to build a retirement income that we can depend on. The various types of financial products available today make up what I like to call the "financial toolbox." Before we start the planning process, we want to make sure we have access to all available tools. We should not arbitrarily exclude certain types of financial tools or asset classes because we think we will not need them; we want to start with a complete toolbox.

The Pros and Cons of Red and Green Tools

To simplify the overwhelming variety of financial tools, I find it helpful to divide the large financial toolbox into two categories. Let's call the first category "red financial tools," and the second category "green financial tools."

All the red tools have an element of market risk with no guarantees. All green tools do not have market risk and do come with certain guarantees. Red = Market Risk. Green = No Market Risk.

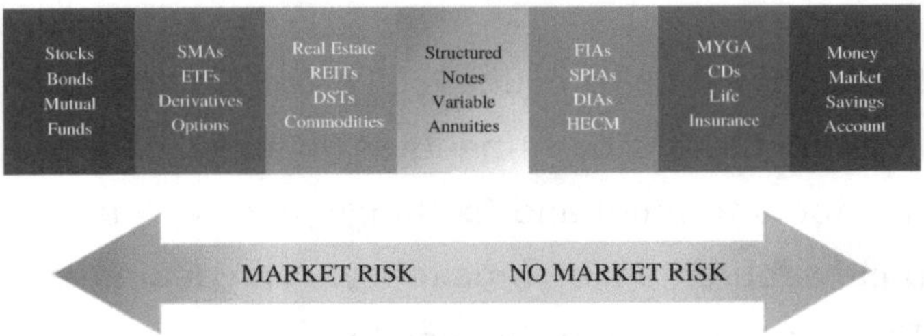

Both red and green tools have unique strengths and weaknesses, pros and cons. There are trade- offs that need to be weighed and considered.

The broad financial services industry is generally made up of advisors and financial companies that solely specialize in either "red tools only" or "green tools only." The two camps come from two different schools of thought and tend to have a strong bias. It is common to see both types demonize the other like fierce competitors. This bias is confusing, unhealthy, and problematic for consumers because it limits their possible solutions and outcomes. The two camps have different licensing, training, and educational requirements.

The "red tools only" folks have long advocated the traditional asset allocation model using primarily mutual funds. The "green tools only" folks focus on insurance-based products with guarantees such as annuities and life insurance.

If an advisor or their firm limits the type of financial tools they use to only half of the financial tools available, how can they be trusted to deliver the best possible strategies needed for many unique and specific situations? Are we forced to decide between using solely green tools or solely red tools, or could we possibly utilize the strengths of each?

True Holistic Retirement Planners Will Have a "Whole" Financial Toolbox

You should be aware that the overwhelming majority of financial firms and advisors in both the red camp and the green camp are not retirement income planners, and their approach is certainly not holistic. As mentioned in Chapter 1, we live in a transaction-based world. The financial advice we are accustomed to receiving from advisors, and most advisors are accustomed to giving, is limited in scope, uncorrelated, and derived from transaction-based advice and services.

A salesperson who works for a hammer manufacturer may make a strong case that a hammer is the best tool of all tools, and a salesperson working for a screwdriver manufacturer may make a strong case about how vitally important it is to have a screwdriver. Which perspective is correct?

If the problem that needs fixing includes measuring and cutting several boards, then neither the hammer nor the screwdriver has the necessary attributes needed for the job. The hammer and screwdriver are not bad tools, they are just not the right tools for that specific job. It is the same with financial tools.

A home builder cannot build a house with only one tool. All the right tools are needed and when they are used with skill and in harmony with each other, the end result is a beautiful home that can provide shelter and comfort.

The full spectrum of financial products available today, both red and green, should be thought of as different types of tools with unique differences and abilities. The best tools capable of fixing our problems depend upon what those specific problems are, not upon what an advisor happens to offer.

A True Fiduciary Advisor Will Be Non-Biased

It is important to make sure that the general contractor working on your retirement plan has the full spectrum of tools and the skills to build a comprehensive and holistic plan that will provide you maximum income and peace of mind throughout retirement. Advisors who are biased toward their financial tools tend to emphasize and exaggerate the strengths of the tools they understand and can sell while overstating the weaknesses of the tools they never use. No doubt you have heard horror stories or rumors about certain types of investments or financial products that turned out to be a financial disaster. Having "quality" tools is very important, but even high-quality tools, if used inappropriately, can be financially disastrous.

Financial Tools Used Inappropriately Can Cause Financial Harm

A chainsaw is an amazing invention, and it can be a very useful tool. If we had a big storm with strong winds during the night and we woke up to a downed tree blocking our street, a chainsaw would be very useful in removing the tree and clearing the road. The tree could be removed the old-fashioned way by using a hand saw or an axe, but with much less efficiency.

As impressive and powerful as a chainsaw is, it can also be extremely dangerous if misused or used without the proper safety gear. The reality is, many people have been severely injured, losing both life and limb while operating a chainsaw. Such a powerful tool requires respect and skill to be used safely and effectively. It is the same with all financial tools. When someone has a bad experience or is financially injured by a certain type of financial tool, there is a tendency to dislike the tool. It is important to realize, however, that it may have had more to do with how the tool was used, or rather misused, and not the tool in and of itself.

Now, just to be clear, I am not saying there aren't some bad financial tools out there too. There are! In these cases, the tools are never as effective no matter how they are used. Some examples of these will be discussed in the coming chapters. They weren't necessarily always bad, but many of them have become bad over time, and they are now rusty and outdated. The world changed, our financial environment changed, technology changed, and they didn't keep up. The problem is many advisors have not kept up either and are still giving the same old advice and using the same old tools. It's much more than just a matter of staying current; it is largely based on their entire business model or career path that was built on a platform that has become outdated over time. For example, if a business and its employees were highly skilled at manufacturing typewriters in the 1970s, it doesn't really matter how expert they were because innovation completely replaced them. Transitioning and adapting to change can be extremely difficult for large companies that were built upon concepts that have become outdated.

One Size Does Not Fit All

I know and respect many qualified financial professionals, but some broker-dealers and/or insurance agencies have a "one size fits all" mentality. They will sell their product to anyone willing to buy on a transactional basis with little regard for the overall best strategy for their client.

Consider a visit to a doctor's office. They check all the vital signs and complete a thorough examination to evaluate and diagnose a patient's health condition before prescribing a treatment plan. Medical doctors have a fiduciary responsibility to do what is in the best interest of the patient. Medication that may be perfect for one patient could be life threatening for a different patient. Similarly, a specific financial product may be a perfect fit for one person, but when used inappropriately, can be a complete disaster for another person. Everyone's situation is unique, so proper comprehensive planning with the right mix of financial tools is the key.

The Fiduciary Standard

The fiduciary standard is required within the attorney/client relationship as well as the doctor/patient relationship, but with financial advisors, it remains optional. A remarkably small percentage of advisors today choose to adhere to the fiduciary standard of care. Most broker-dealers and their registered reps, as well as most insurance agents, are not fiduciaries and they are definitely not holistic planners.

The fiduciary standard of care requires that a financial advisor act solely in the client's best interest when offering personalized financial advice.

A fiduciary has a legal responsibility and obligation to fulfill. I must ask, why would anyone trust their life savings with an advisor who is unwilling to make the legally binding commitment to do what is in the best interest of the client?

There are many good and ethical non-fiduciary financial advisors. I personally know many, but in our competitive world, why settle for less than the highest standard?

It's important to remember that working with a fiduciary does not necessarily guarantee that they are good at what they do, nor does it suggest that they are skilled holistic planners.

There are some popular "red tools only" firms that emphasize in their advertising that they are fiduciaries and at the same time they arbitrarily exclude all "green tools." How can they claim to do what is in the best interest of the client when they have an incomplete financial toolbox with which to work? How can an honest advisor who says they are going to act on what is in the client's best interest exclude an entire asset class and its unique set of attributes, before they know anything about the client's specific needs?

Generalizations Are Usually Misleading and Inaccurate

Broad generalizations are always unreliable and full of inaccuracies. Racism and prejudice happen by putting people into a generalized box and attaching a label to that box. To label an entire race or religion of people as being bad or good is ridiculous! People are unique individuals with their own personal strengths and weaknesses. The color of one's skin has absolutely nothing to do with the content of their character. Just as good and bad characters can be found in every race and religion, good and bad attributes can be found in every asset class (financial tools).

Beware of financial firms or advisors that make broad generalizations. There is far too much complexity and innovation within the financial services industry to make general assumptions based on the past.

Only a small percentage of today's financial advisors are fiduciaries with a full toolbox and the holistic planning skills necessary to get the job done right. A quality plan will often use a strategic combination of red and green tools customized to best meet the needs of the individual or couple.

Summary:

- We need the benefits that financial institutions can provide.
- Inflation decreases our buying power over time, and achieving growth is vital.
- Attributes of the perfect investment are not found in any one financial product.
- The right combination of financial products is an important part of holistic planning.
- Both red and green tools have strengths and weaknesses to be considered.
- True holistic retirement planners will have a complete financial toolbox.
- A true fiduciary advisor will not have a bias toward any one financial tool.
- Financial tools used inappropriately can cause financial harm.
- Every situation is unique. One size does not fit all.
- Generalizations are often misleading and inaccurate.

Chapter 7

Investments (Red Financial Tools)

Markets Are Unpredictable

The "red financial tools" within our financial toolbox includes a mind-numbing variety of investment choices within the investment industry.

As we approach our retirement years, preservation of assets becomes increasingly important. How much market risk should you assume? How much is too much and how much might be too little? Market-based investments are unpredictable and will always fluctuate. Nobody knows what the news events will be tomorrow or next week, and nobody can predict what the markets will do. In a letter to Berkshire Hathaway shareholders, Warren Buffett said: "The years ahead will occasionally deliver major market declines—even panics—that will affect virtually all stocks. No one can tell you when these traumas will occur."

In Chapter 5, we discussed the risks and challenges associated with traditional asset allocation and the reduced income that can be safely withdrawn from a portfolio when using low interest bonds. In recent years, excellent alternatives to bonds (green tools), with the ability to produce more predictable income than bonds, have become available and will be explored in the coming chapters. In this chapter, we will discuss market-based investments (red tools).

The Growth Potential of Stocks

Stocks are important as they have historically offered the most potential for growth. Professor of finance, *Dr. Jeremy Siegel*, PhD at The Wharton School of the University of Pennsylvania, did a study of the returns of different types of assets over the past 200 years. Stocks are the unquestioned leader with a 200-year average return of 6.7%. Bonds came in second at 3.5%, then T-Bills at 2.7%. Gold came in at 0.5% and the dollar at -1.4%. Managing our exposure to the stock market is vital, and the investment strategy used can make or break a retirement plan.

Investment Platforms

Let's take a big picture view of the investment platforms available. I use the term "investment platform" to reference the different formats available in which you can use to invest, not the actual investments.

For example, if we were talking about professional sports, the platform for an NBA game would include a hardwood floor, a basketball, and hoops with nets on each end of the court. The NFL operates on a different platform, using a much larger area of grass or turf, helmets, and an oval- shaped ball. The NHL operates within yet another platform that includes sticks, pucks, and a large sheet of ice. These three platforms are all associated with professional sports and each platform is uniquely different from the others. We are not talking about any specific teams or players—only the difference in the structure or environment in which they operate.

There are four distinct investment platforms that we will review in this chapter: DIY, mutual funds, ETFs, and SMAs.

Investment Platform #1

D.I.Y.

This is the Do-It-Yourself platform. With this approach you use an online brokerage account and make your own investments and trades. You watch the financial news, you sign up to receive stock tips, and you do your best to pick the winners and time the market.

Statistically, this approach is the absolute worst approach you can take. Even if you have a burning desire to do it yourself, the statistics are overwhelmingly against you.

Only a very small percentage of serious do-it-yourselfers have success. Occasionally, a day trader will get lucky, and everyone hears about it. It's like going to a casino: Most people lose but occasionally someone hits the jackpot, and it makes the news. Gambling with your retirement nest egg is a bad idea.

Emotions get in the way with this approach. While everyone hopes to buy low and sell high, they end up doing the exact opposite. There is compelling evidence and studies that clearly document this fact. Over time and on average, the do-it-yourselfers experience greater losses and underperform in the market. If you have been doing some trading on your own and just can't seem to resist the thrill, it is generally recommended that you limit your trading to a small percentage of your nest egg.

Investment Platform #2

Mutual Funds

Mutual funds were once an effective platform, but that is no longer the case. They first began in the 1920s, when it was difficult for the everyday consumer to access a diversified investment portfolio. Humble account balances were limited to the low earnings of a savings account at the local bank. Mutual funds solved a problem and provided a retail investment platform that offered easy access to potentially higher returns of stocks and bonds. Mutual funds are like pre-packaged "off the shelf" investment portfolios that simplified the process and opened a world of investing to many that had never invested before.

In the early years, there were only a handful of mutual funds compared to the tens of thousands available today. Fund managers also had more flexibility regarding investment decisions. The successful fund managers gained respect and popularity over other less successful managers. As the demand for mutual funds increased, the industry developed more of a team management approach to avoid being too dependent upon only a few well-known investment managers.

As the industry grew, the number of mutual funds increased significantly. New mutual fund companies became more focused on niche products, which resulted in less flexibility for fund managers as well as more complicated fee structures.

Growth of the Mutual Fund Industry

We experienced incredible bull markets during the 80s and 90s. It almost didn't matter how you invested because the market experienced sustained growth for nearly two decades. During this time, the mutual fund industry grew into a gigantic multi trillion-dollar industry. The mutual fund investment platform became the standard for the individual investor. In 1980, the first 401k plan was born when the Johnson

Companies became the first company to offer a 401k plan to its employees. The name comes from section 401k of the Internal Revenue Code which came into existence with the passing of the Revenue Act of 1978. In 1981, the IRS issued new rules that permitted an employer to offer a retirement plan to which employees may contribute a portion of their wages on a pretax basis.

The 401k contribution plans were less expensive for employers, and they provided an opportunity to lower their overhead costs. To be competitive, companies started to adopt 401k plans as an alternative to the more expensive pension plans.

The investment options within a 401k plan are, for the most part, a list of mutual funds. Again, the mutual fund platform was convenient and simplified the investment options available to 401k plan participants. Today, trillions of dollars are invested in mutual funds.

Mutual Funds: No Transparency

The platform upon which mutual funds are built is outdated and full of flaws. When you buy a mutual fund, you don't own any stocks or bonds, rather you own a claim on the holdings within the fund and the mutual fund owns the actual equities. It is a cumbrous arrangement, and it adds complexity and inefficiencies that are both costly and unnecessary.

Most mutual fund investors have no idea how much they are paying in fees and expenses. The known fees are disclosed and have many names, such as loads, sales charges, commissions, 12b-1 fees, redemption fees, management fees, and deferred sales charges. If you have a portfolio made up of many mutual funds, each fund will have its own expense ratio and costs making it difficult for an investor to sort it all out.

The unknown costs inherent in the mutual fund platform are **not** disclosed! You may be aware that mutual funds have "hidden costs;" however, they are more often a result of the complexity and inefficiencies within the platform itself and have less to do with the sneaky behavior of the mutual fund companies. Don't get me wrong, there is plenty of sneaky business that goes on, such as "window dressing" and "leaning for the tape." These typically occur just before the quarterly report gets published to make the fund management look better than it truly is. This stuff happens, and it is made possible due to the opaque nature of mutual funds.

Many of the costs within a mutual fund are not known in advance and are difficult to predict, making it impossible to reveal total actual costs. If you look at a mutual fund prospectus, you will see the breakdown of "disclosed fees." However, if you look further in the fine print, you will also find reference to the fact that there are "other expenses" associated with portfolio turnover, transaction costs, and embedded capital gains taxes that are not disclosed and they definitely have a negative impact on the fund's performance.

Price Impact, Bid-Ask Spreads, and Adverse Selection

When mutual funds buy stocks on behalf of the fund, they are typically large transactions in the millions of dollars for a single stock. Popular mutual funds are exceptionally large and manage billions of dollars in one fund. If a fund wants to buy millions of shares of XYZ stock priced at $32 per share, they often cannot get all the shares they want at that price because of price impact, bid-ask spreads, and adverse selection, which drives up the price artificially. These terms may be unfamiliar, but simply put, they translate into additional costs and inefficiencies that negatively impact the performance of a fund.

Unknown and Undisclosed Costs

The undisclosed costs within mutual funds are real and they are shared by everyone who has a claim on the fund. You **cannot** uncover the true costs of a mutual fund by analyzing the mutual fund's prospectus only. You will also need to understand and breakdown the fund's annual report to the board members. If you have many mutual funds in your portfolio you will need to do the same analysis for each mutual fund. Virtually NOBODY does that, and nobody knows the true costs within their mutual funds. Whatever you think your total mutual fund costs are, if you double or triple that number, you are likely getting close.

How Much Do Mutual Funds Really Cost?

Mutual Funds Average Costs
Disclosed Expense Ratio 1.19%
Hidden Costs 1.44%
Costs due to tax inefficiency 1.10%
Costs due to sneaky behavior 2.49%
Total Costs 6.22%

"According to several academic studies published by finance professors at institutions such as the University of Texas at Austin, University of Virginia, University of Missouri, and Georgia State University, the additional cost due to mutual funds' sneaky behaviors is 2.49%."

"How Much Do Mutual Funds Really Cost?" Forbes, originally published September 24, 2016, updated June 29, 2021.

Mutual Fund Overlap

The inherent costs within a mutual fund are not the only problem. An investment portfolio with many mutual funds will almost certainly have "duplication," referred to as mutual fund overlap. This is when multiple mutual funds contain several of the same stocks in their underlying holdings. When doing a portfolio analysis for a prospective client, it is common for me to see that multiple stocks were purchased multiple times by separate mutual funds within the client's portfolio. You only need to buy a stock once! It is wasteful to pay for transaction costs multiple times, which is what happens within a portfolio of mutual funds.

Diversification is important, but a portfolio made up of many mutual funds is not the answer.

Duplication not only creates additional costs. It also increases the risk level of the portfolio because you are not as diversified as you think you are when you have overlap.

Performance Drag

All these inefficiencies within the mutual fund platform result in performance drag. It is like having a "ball and chain" tethered to your portfolio holding it back. The underperformance of mutual funds on a large scale is a well- known statistical fact within the industry, but the multi trillion-dollar mutual fund industry, for obvious reasons, prefers to maintain the status quo. Although the industry has deep pockets and a strong hold on trillions of assets, there is an exodus taking place as investors become more aware of better options. Large sums of money are being moved out of mutual funds and into more transparent and efficient platforms.

To be clear, there are low-cost index mutual funds now available that are decent, but still lack the liquidity and transparency of newer platforms.

The mutual fund is a product of the 20th century. The platform is built on an archaic, out-of-date architecture. Welcome to the 21st century where better and more efficient ways to invest are now available!

Investment Platform #3

Exchange Traded Funds (ETFs)

A Revolutionary Platform

Exchange Traded Funds (ETFs) are a much newer platform and have become very popular since the early 2000s. You could think of the ETF as a new and improved mutual fund, but they are built upon an entirely different platform. An ETF can hold a much broader variety of asset classes in addition to stocks and bonds, such as gold and silver, and other commodities, as well as currencies, and now even Bitcoin and other cryptocurrencies. ETFs cover the entire market spectrum, ranging from broad asset classes to specialty markets, sectors, and factors. The ETF has revolutionized the approach to diversified investing and the efficiency, precision, and sophistication for all types of investors.

Typically, an ETF will replicate an index by purchasing the same stocks or bonds that make up a market index or combination of indexes. For example, you could purchase an ETF that closely mirrors the performance of the S&P 500. With one ETF you could own the entire index.

ETFs: Transparency and Cost Efficiency

ETFs do not have the embedded capital gains problem found in mutual funds. ETFs are transparent and cost efficient. One of the distinct advantages of ETFs over mutual funds is their liquidity and intra- day trading. An ETF can be bought and sold on an exchange just the same as an individual stock. This is quite different from the slow and cumbersome structure of mutual funds as they are not traded on exchanges and cannot be liquidated until the end of the trading day.

ETFs: Popularity and Growth

According to a 2024 study by JP Morgan, "As of the end of May 2024, there were around 3,500 ETFs listed in the U.S., which held approximately $9 trillion in assets" for the US. Globally 12,000 ETFs and $13T AUM

https://www.jpmorgan.com/insights/global-research/investing/etf-guide

Actively managed mutual funds seek to outperform the market and, statistically speaking, it just does not happen. There are many studies and data that show this reality with great clarity. According to

Morningstar data, more than 88% of all U.S. mutual funds underperform their market benchmarks! If actively managed mutual funds overwhelmingly underperform the market and are more expensive to manage, simply buying a low-cost ETF index fund will ensure that you get whatever the overall market gets or at least very close to it. Most investors do not understand this one fact, which is revolutionary all by itself.

Market Risk Remains

As you can tell, I like ETFs for several reasons. However, for those approaching retirement age, market risk remains a major issue that needs to be addressed. Both the mutual fund platform and the ETF platform are based on a buy-and-hold concept. The buy-and-hold strategy is based on getting on the market rollercoaster and staying on through all the ups and downs. Buy-and-hold is good when you have a long time-horizon, but sequence risk becomes a threat as you near retirement.

The argument for buy-and-hold is based on the importance of not missing out on the market's best days, but it has no defense against the systemic risk and bear markets.

Buy and Hold Argument: What if you missed the Best Days?	
During 1990-2012, the S&P 500's Average Annual Return was 6.18%	
If you missed the....	Your Average Return fell to:
Best 10 Days	3.02%
Best 20 Days	0.92%
Best 30 Days	-0.87%
Best 40 Days	-2.52%

As you can see in the table above, over a 22- year period (1990–2012), the S&P 500 returned an average of 6.18%. If you happen to be out of the market on the market's ten best days, your average return over that time frame would have been reduced by more than half! That right there is the compelling reason to get in and stay in. But what if we were to change our thinking? Instead of seeking the highest gains possible, what if we were able to reduce or even avoid the market's worst days?

Tactical/Defensive Argument: What if you missed the Worst Days?	
During 1990-2012, the S&P 500's Average Annual Return was 6.18%	
If you missed the....	Your Average Return soared to:
Worst 10 Days	9.77%
Worst 20 Days	12.33%
Worst 30 Days	14.55%
Worst 40 Days	16.50%

As you can see, during the same time frame, if we are able to avoid the market's ten worst days, our average return over the same 22-year period has increased to 9.77%! If we can reduce or minimize market losses, we do not have to waste the time it takes to recover from a deep market loss. So, how do we do that?

Investment Platform #4

Separately Managed Accounts (SMAs) and Buffered ETFs

While the ETF platform by itself has many advantages over the mutual fund platform, there is a platform that utilizes publicly traded ETFs and stocks as well as private equity markets that I believe provides a superior investment solution: SMAs.

What is the SMA platform?

Institutional investors have had many advantages not available to individual investors. Large university endowment funds, hedge funds, super wealthy individuals, and many large institutions typically do not invest using the retail platforms most common to middle America (mutual funds). Rather, they have their own professional money managers. These types of accounts are often referred to as "Separately Managed Accounts (SMAs)" or simply "Managed Money."

ETFs and SMAs combined have turned the hedge fund industry on its ear. Hedge funds are only available to high net worth individuals or institutions. Hedge funds charge performance fees in the neighborhood of 20% of gains on top of 2% management fees for strategies that are now available with low cost ETFs and SMAs.

In years past, SMAs were known to have had high minimum investment requirements, and they were simply not available to most people. With the advances in technology and increased demand for better investment options following the 2008 financial crisis, SMAs and buffered ETFs are now available to virtually everyone. More about buffered ETFs in a few pages.

In a Separately Managed Account, securities are owned directly by you. You do not have the problems inherent with mutual funds: no embedded capital gains problems, no hidden costs caused by commingled funds, and no duplication. There are also no inherent conflicts of interest associated with commission or transaction-based investment products. That means no confusing fees, no loads, no sales charges, no redemption fees, and no surrender charges. Of course, SMAs and fiduciary advisors do have fees, but they are typically based on a flat rate percentage of assets under management with the natural incentive to help your money grow over time. You get complete transparency and know exactly what the fees are in advance of making a decision.

Hedging Against Bear Markets

The primary method of traditional portfolio allocation to hedge against bear markets is to include a higher proportion of bonds. Target date funds, popular in employer plans like 401(k)s, are mutual funds that automatically adjust the ratio of stocks to bonds based on a target retirement date, becoming more conservative as the target date approaches. However, one major problem with this approach is the assumption that bonds are inherently conservative or defensive. More on bonds later.

As previously mentioned, a young investor with a long time-horizon may have time to recover from a deep market loss. Those of us, however, approaching retirement age or already in retirement cannot afford to lose 40%- 50% of our portfolio as was experienced during the periods from 2000-2002 and 2007-2009.

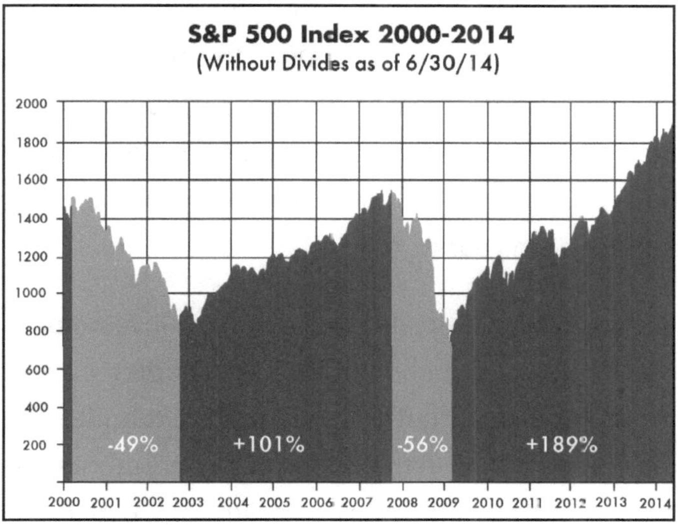

To further demonstrate the profound realization of the difference between the decades of the 1990s and the 2000s, note the following illustration of a hypothetical investment in the S&P 500 Index for the indicated time periods:

Time Period	Account Value:	Account Value:
Jan 1, 1990 – Dec 31, 1999	1/1/1990: **$100,000**	12/31/1999: **$423,700**
Jan 1, 2000 – Dec 31, 2009	1/1/2000: **$100,000**	12/31/2009: **$79,970**

Wow! What a contrast. $100,000 growing to $423,700 during the 90s versus $100,000 being reduced to only $79,970 during the 2000s. The buy-and-hold strategy worked like a charm during the 80s and 90s but failed miserably during the 2000s. You would have done better with money under your mattress for those ten years!

How can we be more defensive with our investments (red tools)? As demonstrated in Chapter 4, it is more important "not to lose" money than it is to take on more risk in the hopes of higher returns. All offense and no defense is a poor strategy, especially when we are nearing retirement age. The goal is to "preserve" and "grow" the assets from prolonged bear market declines.

Buffered ETFs

Buffered ETFs are ETFs with a structured outcome, or you might say a defined outcome. They are a relatively recent innovation in the realm of exchange-traded funds (ETFs).

Buffered ETFs didn't exist prior to the 2008 market crash. The innovation came from an increased investor demand for products that offered some form of downside protection while still participating in potential market gains.

The concept is rooted in structured products that have been around for many decades in traditional financial markets such as structured bank notes. A buffered ETF is a structured product that has been integrated with an ETF to provide greater accessibility, transparency, and liquidity.

A buffered ETF is an exchange-traded fund designed to offer downside protection while participating in the upside of a market index. It does this by providing a buffer against a predetermined range of losses while allowing for gains up to a certain limit.

ETFs utilize a reference index (like the S&P 500) and a return index to create a predefined range within which the ETF will perform. Using simpler language, it's like setting up guardrails on your investments to better manage risk and limit exposure to extreme market volatility.

There are many different types of structured banknotes, and they can be an important component of a portfolio, but they are not listed on securities exchanges and have much less liquidity than buffered ETFs.

Alternative Investments and Private Equity

Diversification is a fundamental principle in portfolio management, aiming to balance risk and reward. Traditionally, portfolios have relied on diversification to minimize risk and enhance returns. However, this strategy doesn't always work as planned. Many traditional investments today are "correlated," meaning they tend to rise or fall together. Correlation gauges the extent to which investments move in the same direction. While stocks and bonds are typically seen as uncorrelated, their correlations can shift, leading to unexpected outcomes.

For example, in 2022, both stocks and bonds experienced declines at the same time. In August

2023, I came across a Bloomberg headline that read, "Bonds are a useless hedge for stock losses as correlation jumps.*" The article pointed out that the correlation between stocks and treasury bonds had reached its highest level since 1996. The problem is that many traditional strategies now focus on adding more investments that are positively correlated, which diminishes the effectiveness of diversification.

This is particularly concerning for older Americans, especially those in or near retirement, who are increasingly avoiding bonds and instead placing the bulk of their future financial security in stocks. This approach carries substantial risk.

The key to an ideal portfolio lies in true diversification, which includes eight to twelve uncorrelated investments. Such a portfolio can significantly reduce risk without compromising potential returns. By carefully structuring a portfolio this way, investors can achieve similar upside potential while reducing the overall risk exposure.

It's worth noting that the number of publicly traded U.S. companies has nearly halved since 1996, leaving around 4,400 companies for investors to consider. With this increased concentration the typical or traditional portfolio has more inherent risk than most realize.

To achieve genuine diversification, it's essential to look beyond public stocks and incorporate alternative investments and private equity. In today's landscape, many companies opt to remain private rather than go public, as they can access capital without the complex regulatory hurdles involved in becoming publicly traded. There are thousands of private companies that are growing, innovating, and disrupting markets. In fact, around 80% of companies generating over $100 million in revenue are privately held. When you compare the total market value of publicly traded companies globally, you'll find that the value of companies in private equity funds surpasses the value of public stocks by nearly four to one.

That said, public stocks still play an important role in a well-diversified portfolio, including my own. However, many investors have not had access to private equity, which is where diversification truly begins to shine.

Numerous studies suggest that incorporating private equity into a traditional stock-and-bond portfolio not only reduces volatility but can also enhance returns.** Ultimately, the goal is to lower risk while increasing potential returns.

*https://www.bloomberg.com/news/articles/2023-08-02/bonds-are-useless-hedge-for-stock-losses-as-correlation-jumps

**https://www.nb.com/en/global/insights/investment-quarterly-asset-matters-private-equity-and-your-portfolio

Predicting the Markets

Nobody can "predict" what the markets will or will not do in the future. Nobody knows what tomorrow's news headlines will read and no prediction will be dependable. But the fact remains that we need our money to grow over time to maintain its buying power. Red investment tools are an indispensable hedge against inflation, but the associated market risks need to be well managed.

Why Don't More People Know About Separately Managed Accounts?

This type of investment management has not been available to the average investor primarily because of previous high minimum requirements. However, this is one of the big changes of the 21st century! With advances in technology, SMAs have become available to most everyone outside of company sponsored plans. This is a big deal, but most people are unaware and don't understand the differences for a few reasons:

1. Availability to the average investor is relatively new.
2. The mutual fund industry maintains a strong hold and influence.
3. SMAs are still not available within employer sponsored plans, such as the 401k.
4. The majority of investment advisors are stuck on the traditions of the past and change is difficult for large firms.

Managed money has an investment advisory fee-based structure, which is transparent and competitive. If you are looking for the lowest possible fees, then you will find them in ETFs. But be careful that you don't strain at a gnat and swallow the volatility camel. You definitely don't want to pay excessive fees, but remember, the single biggest expense with investing is not the fees, but rather the costs associated with market volatility, which we demonstrated in Chapter 5.

In conclusion, the mutual fund platform was once an effective investment platform but is outdated, and far better options are now available. Just as the horse and buggy were once the best form of transportation, innovation and technology has brought about far better forms of transportation.

Summary:

- Markets are unpredictable and risk must be properly managed.
- Historically, stocks have provided the best potential for growth.
- Understanding the difference between investment platforms is important.
- Investment Platform #1: D.I.Y.
- Investment Platform #2: Mutual funds
- Mutual funds are opaque and do not provide transparency.
- Price impact, bid-ask spreads, and adverse selection contribute to underperformance.
- Total mutual fund costs are unknown and undisclosed.

- The real cost of owning a mutual fund is more than most realize.
- Mutual fund overlap is a common problem with mutual fund portfolios.
- Capital gains tax and many other issues cause performance drag.
- <u>Investment Platform #3:</u> Exchange Traded Funds (ETFs)
- The ETF is a revolutionary new investment platform.
- ETFs are transparent, highly liquid, and cost efficient.
- ETFs continue to increase in popularity.
- True diversification cannot be fully achieved without incorporating alternative investments and private equity.
- <u>Investment Platform #4:</u> Separately Managed Accounts (SMAs)
- SMAs: A superior platform is now available.
- The majority of actively managed mutual funds underperform their market benchmark.

Chapter 8

Annuities and Life Insurance (Green Financial Tools)

21st Century Innovation

"Everything that can be invented has been invented." This is the infamous quote of Charles H. Duell, the Commissioner of US patent office back in 1899. I'm sure most people living in the 19th century could hardly imagine the innovation and advances that took place during the 20th century. And now, in just the first two decades of the 21st century alone, innovation has been nothing short of remarkable.

As a boy in the 70s, I remember imagining what it would be like to have a cordless telephone that you could take with you anywhere. It seemed too good to be true. Fast forward to present day: I can use my smart phone to do that and infinitely more. From anywhere in the world, I can see who is at my doorstep and speak to them. I can unlock the front door, open and lower my garage door, adjust the thermostat, and have face-to-face video calls with family members living in other states. I can order virtually any product and expect it to arrive on my doorstep in 24 hours or less. I can take a photo or record a video and publish it around the world within seconds. I can pay bills, make deposits, transfer money, and never have to wait in line at the bank.

We now have self-driving cars available in some cities. We will soon be able to order an Uber drone that will fly you across town when we need to get somewhere quickly. Yes, flying taxis are just around the corner; the futuristic day of the Jetsons has arrived. Innovation has, and will continue to, change the quality of our lives.

Innovation is found in all industries, including the financial services industry. In Chapter 7, we learned about the birth and growth of Exchange Traded Funds and new access to Separately Managed Accounts. These are 21st century improvements and are the direct result of innovation.

Guarantees and No Market Risk

"Green financial tools" are financial products that come with guarantees and have no market risk. There has been little innovation with a basic savings account and certificates of deposit which would be considered green tools and are available at the local bank. The insurance-based products, including annuities and life insurance, however, have evolved and transformed with remarkable 21st century innovation.

The History of Annuities

Annuities have been around for centuries. Believe it or not, archeological evidence of annuities dates back to Babylon in 2500 B. C., Egypt in 1100 B. C., and within the Roman Empire in the second and third centuries A. D. The first annuity was offered in America in 1759 by a company in Pennsylvania for Presbyterian ministers and their families. Ministers could contribute to a fund in exchange for lifetime payments. After the 1929 market crash, the demand grew for financial products that offered guarantees.

The basic concept of an annuity is a sum of money paid to someone on a monthly or yearly basis, typically for the rest of their life. A company pension is basically an employer sponsored annuity. Social Security is a big public annuity funded through taxes. Personal asset-based annuities are provided and guaranteed by insurance companies.

The annuity world is vast. There are many different annuity products available with a host of features, configurations, and benefits. Annuities are an important tool in retirement income planning that can be used for various reasons and can solve many financial problems. Evolution and innovation have made annuities more and more effective and beneficial. As with any tool, annuities should be used appropriately and with skill.

Types of Annuities: Fixed, Variable, and Fixed Index

The oldest and most basic type of annuity is a fixed annuity. A fixed annuity generally comes with a guaranteed fixed interest rate while guaranteeing the principal investment. The problem with fixed annuities is that the interest rates are generally low and not as exciting as market-based investments. As the industry looked for ways to improve annuities and bring together the benefits of market-based investments, as well as the benefits of an annuity, led to the creation of the variable annuity in the mid-20th century.

The concept of the variable annuity is not a bad concept. It is based on investments subject to market risk that can lose value but with a minimum guarantee offered by the annuity company. The variable annuity structure, however, has multiple components, including investments similar to mutual funds called "sub accounts." These have their own fees and inefficiencies, as well as increased administrative costs from the annuity company. They are burdened with layers of fees in the range of 2.75% to 3.5%. I have even seen some as high as 4%. This creates a tremendous drag on the investment account and explains, in part, their underperformance.

When I referred to outdated and rusty old financial tools, this would be one of them. When negative stories are told about annuities, they are most often referring to variable annuities. The problem is many broker/dealers are still promoting them.

The idea behind a variable annuity is that the investments in them have a chance of growing above the minimum guarantees offered by the annuity company, but in my experience, it rarely does.

I don't love variable annuities but something amazing has happened in the 21st century: the development of Fixed Index Annuities (FIAs).

Fixed-Index Annuities (FIAs)

Imagine if there was a place you could put some of your retirement nest egg that had zero downside market risk, zero fees, tax advantages, and your money could grow based on the upside performance of a market index such as the S&P 500. It sounds almost too good to be true, and you may be wondering if such a place really exists. Yes, it is called a Fixed-Index Annuity and it is a game-changer for soon- to-be retirees.

The FIAs available today did not exist during the 20th century. The birth of the first FIA was in 1995, but they were in their infancy and hardly anybody knew about them.

Within the first five years, at the turn of the century, the number of carriers offering FIAs had grown from 1 to 50. As the advantages of FIAs became better known and understood during the mid-2000s, the consumer demand continued to grow. After the 2008 financial crisis, FIA growth soared with billions of dollars moving into FIAs every year. Today, total FIA assets are in the trillions and growing rapidly.

A Financial Tool with Unique Attributes

The advantages of FIAs are truly revolutionary with their guaranteed principal, and the new potential for growth tied to a market index at either no cost or very low cost, depending upon the specific annuity.

Just as the first automobiles were nothing like the automobiles available today, the FIA innovation has continued each year. They have further improved with more flexibility and problem-solving abilities.

Innovative Indexing Strategies

Much of the research and innovation has been focused on new and better indexing strategies within the FIAs.

There are many different index crediting methods and combinations of methods to choose from. But the basic concept is that if a market index like the

S&P 500 goes up, then you enjoy upside growth. If the market goes negative, you are guaranteed to never lose money due to market losses.

With a Fixed-Index Annuity, you will never get all the stock market gains, but you also never get any of the losses. This means you will never waste time trying to recover from a market loss. If you remember from Chapter 4, we demonstrated how volatility is enemy #1 and can damage your nest egg, especially in retirement when negative sequence becomes a threat. Again, not losing money is more important than chasing after the highest gains possible.

Having said that, there are some remarkable breakthroughs in recent years with uncapped index strategies that have amazing potential for growth. One such index was designed by Roger Ibbotson, PhD., a professor at Yale University, who has helped to change the way investors think about investment allocations, especially for those nearing retirement age.

FIAs: An Excellent Alternative to Bonds

Now, annuities are not in competition with mutual funds or other "red financial tools." It is important to know that you would never want to put all your retirement assets into a FIA. We are only talking about a portion of your retirement nest egg. In Chapter 5, we pointed out that with traditional asset allocation, you will need a combination of stocks and bonds. You can't afford to take on too much risk as you head into retirement. Therefore, if you follow the outdated traditional asset allocation portfolio model, you are going to end up with between 40% to 60% of bonds in your portfolio.

Hope is Not a Strategy

The traditional asset allocation model is an investment strategy, but it is not a retirement income strategy! It has no safety net, and it relies solely on market growth. It requires a lot of hope in more risky "red" markets. It is important to remember that hope is not a strategy.

Bonds are generally considered less risky than stocks, but they come with no guarantees. Bonds have many risks, and they lose value in an increasing interest rate environment.

The Bond Bull Market Has Ended

In recent years, massive losses were experienced by bond holders, both individuals and institutions. The collapse of the Silicon Valley bank and other banks were directly tied to their large holding of bonds in an inflationary environment.

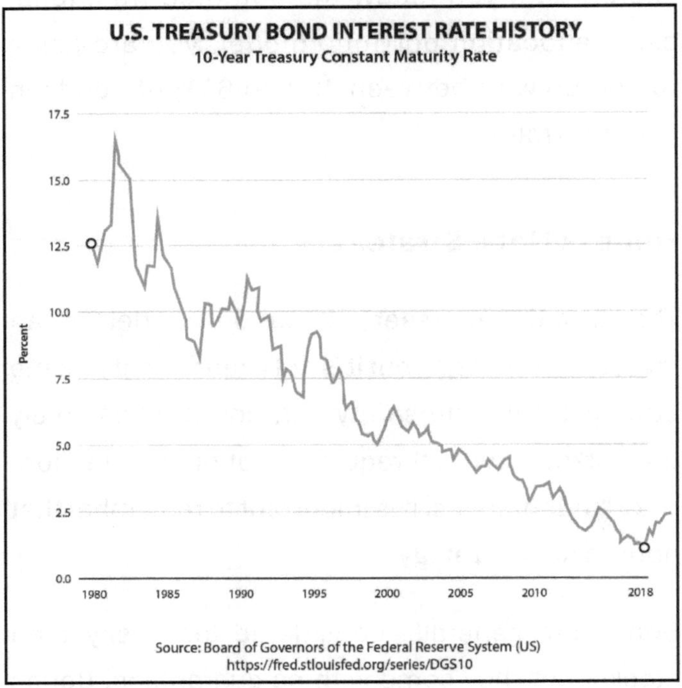

For many people heading into retirement, bonds do not even belong in their retirement portfolio! How is that for a revolutionary statement? An FIA is an excellent alternative to bonds and can provide better growth and stability than bonds.

Now, I have not even mentioned one of the greatest strengths and advantages of annuities, and that is the guaranteed income stream for life.

One of the risks that could cause you to run short of money in retirement is longevity risk. As explained in Chapter 5, longevity is a risk multiplier because the longer you live, the more money you will need, and you have more time for all other risks to become a problem. FIAs can solve the longevity problem with guaranteed income for life.

Creating More Income with FIAs

What if you could get $100,000 to do the work of $200,000 or even $300,000, depending upon the length of retirement?

With traditional asset allocation, you spend principal and interest. With a guaranteed income stream from an annuity, you spend principal, interest, and "mortality credits." Mortality credits are additional income dollars that can be paid to you above and beyond the principal and interest. The additional dollars are based on the guarantees of the issuing insurance company.

When we use an income annuity as part of a retirement income plan, we are combining actuarial science and investments. Actuarial science is based on the law of large numbers. The insurance companies know how long people will live, on average, as a large group. Some live longer than others, but the average is known. Based on that information, insurance companies can provide guaranteed income for life, regardless of how long you live. Even if you deplete your assets, the income stream just keeps flowing for as long as you live: It's guaranteed. Mortality credits, also known as mortality yield, are the terms that refer to the income received after funds have been depleted.

With an income annuity, we can create leverage. As discussed in Chapter 5, with traditional asset allocation, the safe withdrawal rate is no longer 4%, but only about 3%. That means for every $100,000 in your portfolio, you can safely withdrawal only $3,000 of income per year without the risk of running out of money prematurely. However, with a guaranteed lifetime income stream from a good annuity, the withdrawal benefit rate may be closer to 5% based on a single life or $5000 of income for every $100,000 in your portfolio.

Annuities can offer income streams based on either a single life or a joint lifetime for spouses. When based on joint lives, the income and mortality credits will continue until the death of the second spouse. The withdrawal benefit rate is around 4.5% for a joint life ($4,500 of income for every $100,000). Depending upon how much time you have before retirement, you may be able to achieve a 5.5% or even 6% withdrawal benefit rate with certain types of deferred FIAs.

The beauty of annuities and actuarial science is that you can take a higher income without the fear of running out prematurely. This is one of the unique attributes that can only be achieved with a green financial tool such as the Fixed-Index Annuity.

Annuity Fees

So, what about fees? Don't annuities have high fees? Variable annuities do, and I would avoid them. However, most FIAs available have either NO fees or LOW fees depending upon optional features.

You may be wondering how an annuity/insurance company can possibly offer a financial product with zero fees. Well, they can, and they do. As discussed in chapter 6, the various types of financial tools each have tradeoffs. They each have their own set of pros and cons. So, what is the tradeoff with FIAs? It is the commitment of time.

An annuity is a long-term contract. Does the insurance company have expenses associated with providing annuities? Yes, of course, but they benefit from managing the assets over an extended period of time, not from charging you fees. It's remarkable how well this works to benefit all parties involved.

You may be wondering how an annuity/insurance company benefits from managing assets. The money managers within an insurance company are some of the best you will find anywhere. They are conservative investors with deep pockets and typically hold large blocks of bonds to maturity. The yield and the numbers are known. A portion of the interest from the bonds is used to buy stock options. If the market goes up, they exercise the option and realize the gains. If the market does not perform, they simply let the option expire. This is how they can pay you interest based on the performance of a market index and also make some money for the insurance company along the way. They can only do it with no fees or low fees when there is a commitment of time.

Understanding Liquidity

What we are talking about here is the liquidity factor. With a FIA, the tradeoff for the benefits provided is a commitment of time and reduced liquidity. Unenlightened annuity critics that live in the "traditional asset allocation ONLY" world, preach with religious fervor to "not lock up your money" in an annuity. So, let's take a closer look at this issue.

First, the idea of maintaining 100% liquidity of your entire retirement portfolio nest egg is not necessary and not at all practical. Often, we are dealing with qualified (pre-tax dollars), and you really don't have full liquidity anyway, because if you pull all the money out in a single year, you would create a very large tax obligation that would bump you up into the higher tax brackets.

Are we not planning for retirement income that spans three decades? If we are using a FIA as part of an overall retirement income plan, and as a bond alternative, then short-term liquidity is not the goal or even a concern. A FIA is best suited for those approaching retirement age and not well suited for those who are still in the early stages of their career.

Built-in Liquidity and Penalty Free Withdrawals

FIA contracts come with early surrender penalties, typically in the first 9 to 12 years, depending upon the specific FIA product chosen. The penalty only applies if you withdraw more than a specified percentage in any given year. FIAs today come with a built-in liquidity amount. In other words, a "penalty free" withdrawal is available each year if you need to pull out additional money early. The percentage that can be withdrawn penalty free during the first 8 to 10 years is typically between 7% to 10% depending upon the specific annuity chosen.

Keep in mind, only a portion of your assets should go into a FIA, not all. You should still have lots of liquidity with your other red investments. If you need to pull out more than 10% of the guaranteed portion of your retirement assets every year, then you did not have a good plan to begin with.

Liquidity needs should be considered and is always a component of a comprehensive retirement income plan. If you want the guarantees, growth, and leverage that can only be provided through actuarial science and FIAs, with either no fees or very low fees, then giving up some liquidity in exchange for the benefits is a very good tradeoff.

Understanding Commissions

What about annuity commissions? Again, the "traditional asset allocation ONLY" advisors will give warnings about high commission products. There is one company in particular which comes to mind. I will not name them, but their marketing message and TV commercials flood the airways and are both incomplete and misleading. There are elements of truth in their advertising and commissions can be a factor, especially for a "green tools only" sales representative, but not for an independent fiduciary retirement planner with a full toolbox of both red and green financial tools.

The insurance companies that offer FIAs compensate representatives out of their own marketing budget typically with a one-time commission. However, there are no fees charged to the client for commissions! This is very different from what most people think of when they hear the word "commissions." If a realtor helps you sell your house, he or she is paid a commission out of the proceeds of the sale. This is not what happens with annuities. There are NO FEES deducted, and your funds are not reduced by even one penny.

Advertisements that suggest you will pay high commissions with annuities are misleading and inaccurate. They suggest that annuities are recommended only because of commission incentives and that the better choice is to put 100% of your assets into their stock and bond mutual funds. To be clear, there are many different FIAs available and some have optional features that may charge a low fee of about 0.95%, but that is optional and often not necessary depending upon your specific needs.

So, how can an insurance company afford to do this? As mentioned, it is due to the long-term nature of an annuity contract and the time the insurance company will have in managing the money. A Certificate of Deposit (CD) at a bank is a similar concept. The longer the term of the CD, the longer the bank has to lend out the money and earn a spread.

The only time you would experience an early surrender penalty is if you deviate from the plan and surrender the CD or the annuity early (within the first 7 to 10 years). With a properly designed plan appropriately aligned with your needs and goals, you should never have to experience the early surrender penalties.

Red Tools Cost More than Green Tools Over Time

Over your retirement lifetime you will pay much more in cumulative fees on red market-based investments than you will with a one-time commission that doesn't even come out of your pocket! This is a fact that the "red tools ONLY" guy fails to point out. Their advertisements suggest they will save you money. The reality is just the opposite!

A fiduciary planner is bound to only do what is in the best interest of the client and is required to be transparent with fees and compensation. A true fiduciary advisor will recommend an appropriate annuity when it is clearly in your best interest to do so.

Annuities are not for everyone, and they are not always a good fit. There are times, however, when the right annuity can be an important component of a retirement income plan, in which case it can provide stability, more retirement income, and peace of mind.

Insurance

Other important green financial tools include various types of insurance for the purpose of managing risk of financial loss. The idea of spreading financial risk by pooling money is ancient and dates back thousands of centuries. You don't want more insurance than necessary, but you also don't want to be exposed to potential risks that could be financially devastating if something unexpected happens. Having the right amount of insurance and the right types to protect our property, health, and family are all key components of a good financial plan.

Insurance can be had for almost anything of value. In 1943, actress Betty Grable was the first celebrity to obtain insurance on her legs through the Lloyd's of London. She had one million dollars of coverage on each leg. In 1953, food critic Egon Ronay insured his taste buds for $400,000 because his livelihood depended upon them. Bruce Springsteen insured his voice for $6 million, and Bob Dylan insured his as well, just in case his voice stops *blowin' in the wind*.

In the balance of this chapter, I will highlight some key points specific to retirement income planning you should be aware of. But first, it is important to understand the history and evolution of life insurance.

Life Insurance

21st century innovation has revolutionized the value and benefits of certain types of life insurance that have become very powerful financial tools for retirees or soon-to-be retirees.

The most common use of life insurance is to provide income protection for a family in the event of the premature death of the breadwinner, especially for those with young children. Term life insurance policies are simple and last for only a specific term, usually 10, 20, or 30 years. When the kids are all grown, and retirement age is approaching, term life insurance policies typically reach the end of their term and many people see little need to keep the coverage in their more mature years.

Permanent life insurance policies are, as the word suggests, permanent. They are not intended for a limited term, but rather for the full balance of your life, which means the death benefit will eventually be paid out to your heirs. In contrast, the percentage of death benefit claims on term policies is around only 1% of policy holders because the terms expire well before average life expectancies.

A distinct difference between a permanent policy and a term policy is a cash value component. In a permanent life insurance policy, a portion of the premium is allocated to the cost of the insurance and another portion is deposited into a cash value side fund within the policy. There are four main types of permanent life insurance: whole life, universal life, universal variable life, and fixed-index universal life.

The Evolution of Policy Types

Whole life insurance has been around for a long time and was the most popular life insurance product from about 1940 to 1970. Whole life policies provide a guaranteed death benefit, guaranteed cash value accumulation, and fixed premiums that don't increase with age.

Whole life policies, in my view, are "out-of-date" because of the low interest rates earned within the cash accumulation account, and also because they have limited flexibility. Universal life, on the other hand, has customizable moving parts, and a lot more flexibility.

Universal life insurance policies (often shortened to UL) are not as old as whole life and they entered the scene in the late 1970s. While whole life policies have seen little innovation or change because of their solid-state structure, UL has had a much greater opportunity to evolve and improve over the years.

UL has evolved similar to annuities. There are three distinct stages of evolution:

1. UL (Universal Life)
2. VUL (Variable Universal Life)
3. FIUL (Fixed Index Universal Life)

The three main differences between the three types of Universal Life are in the way the cash value side accounts grow. UL was the first of its kind. The cash value earns interest based on current interest rates but with a guaranteed minimum interest rate of growth. UL policies are not super exciting as far as growing the cash value, which helped lead to the creation of the VUL.

In the first part of this chapter, we learned about variable annuities and the same type of structure was applied to variable universal life insurance. The VUL is a red financial tool because the cash value is invested into mutual fund-like investments called "sub accounts." The VUL is the marriage between a UL and market-based investments. Again, a nice idea, but VULs are way too risky and inefficient in my opinion. If you experience a deep market drawdown, not only do you lose your money, but you could lose your life insurance policy and the many other benefits at the same time.

A Uniquely Powerful Financial Tool

A modern day, 21st century fixed-index universal life (FIUL) is a powerful financial tool with unique and valuable attributes. FIUL policies can do some things that no other financial tool can do. Now remember, you do not need every tool in the financial tool box, but you do want the right combination of tools and the right attributes tailored to your specific needs.

There are many critics of permanent life insurance and you have probably heard some of their negative opinions, complaints, and the dire warnings to stay away from permanent life insurance policies. Many of the problems in the past originated, in part, from the inflexibility of whole life policies that cannot adjust well to the changing needs of the policy owner. On top of that, many insurance agents (green financial tools ONLY guys) would sell to anyone willing to buy a permanent policy. These are non-fiduciary insurance brokers who did not and do not provide comprehensive financial planning; rather, they are salespeople selling a product. As a result, there have been far too many people who ended up with a policy that was misaligned with their financial needs and goals. Instead of improving their financial position, they were actually worse off. This reminds me of our "chainsaw" analogy. A chainsaw can cause a lot of damage when mishandled, but when in the hands of a skilled professional, it can be an indispensable tool.

Life Insurance Retirement Plan (LIRP)

Fixed-index universal life Insurance, when used in retirement planning, is sometimes referred to as a Life Insurance Retirement Plan (LIRP). A LIRP, when properly designed and customized as one component of many components, can be an essential piece of the retirement planning puzzle.

One of the Greatest Tax Advantages Available

Another benefit of life insurance is that it has one of the best tax advantages in the tax code. The wealthy have used cash value life insurance as a tax shelter for decades. The death benefit is not only an effective way to protect and pass on assets tax free, but the cash value that accumulates inside this type of policy can be accessed tax-free, even while living.

A Tax-Free Retirement

In Chapter 3, we learned about the importance of tax diversification and in having the optimal balance between the three tax buckets in order to achieve a tax- free retirement. Retirement assets for most

Americans are located in the tax-deferred bucket with "yet to be taxed" dollars. We want to use Roth Conversions, Roth IRAs, and Roth 401ks as much as possible but sometimes the proper balance cannot be achieved without using a custom designed LIRP.

Like a Roth, assets held in a LIRP can only get into the bucket with after-tax dollars. Once the money is in this bucket, however, the gains are tax deferred and can be accessed tax-free through guaranteed policy loans. The end result is tax-free growth and tax-free distributions. A LIRP has no RMDs to worry about and the money is immune to increasing tax rates.

How can I say "immune" to increasing taxes? Can't the cash hungry government change the tax laws on life insurance? Although I believe it to be unlikely for a number of reasons, the tax advantages within life insurance could potentially be changed in the future. However, historically when changes have been made, they only applied to new policy holders, while those with existing policies were grandfathered in with the existing rules intact. To make a change that impacts existing policies would be unreasonable and problematic, not to mention politically unpopular.

The same question could be asked about Roth accounts. Hypothetically, lawmakers could choose to eliminate the Roth tax advantages but doing so on existing Roth account holders would result in double taxation, which is highly unlikely. So, in other words, if you have a Roth or a LIRP before any tax laws are changed, you would most likely be grandfathered in and able to keep what you have.

Non-Taxable Retirement Income

If you look at an IRS 1040 form, you will see that it inquires about various sources of income, wages, interest earned, dividend earnings, pension income, rental income, IRA distributions, and others, including Social Security benefits. Of course, they ask all these questions so that they can collect the required taxes. There are two sources of income, though, that are nowhere to be found on the tax form: any account preceded by the word "Roth" and money coming from a life insurance policy.

The only way to get your assets into the "tax-free bucket" are with Roth accounts and cash value life insurance. Not everyone will qualify for life insurance, but sometimes, depending upon your specific financial situation, the only way to achieve a zero percent tax burden in retirement is with a custom designed FIUL policy.

Revolutionary 21st Century Innovation

The tax advantages are not the only desirable attribute found within fixed-index universal life insurance policies. The innovative index crediting strategies that have become available in recent years are a remarkable improvement. Interest is credited to the cash value based on the performance of a market index such as the S&P 500. When the market has gains, you accumulate gains. When the market has losses, you do not lose any money! The worst that can happen in any year is experiencing zero return. Your money within an FIUL is not exposed to market loss. The equity indexing strategies are a breakthrough improvement over the low interest rates of the older types of cash value life insurance.

Potential for Double Digit Gains with Zero Market Risk

Double digit gains may be achieved when the market is up, but you will not get all the market gains because the insurance company is using options (derivatives), which means a FIUL typically will have index caps and/or participation rates. The historical returns average around 7% growth over 15 years. When you don't have to spend time recovering from market losses, your money can grow surprisingly well. Less volatility results in better growth performance.

Where else can you potentially average 7% returns with no market risk? Only with green financial tools such as fixed index universal life insurance and fixed index annuities.

How Safe are Insurance Companies?

The "guarantees" are based on the claims paying ability of the insurance company. The insurance industry is heavily regulated, and insurers are required to maintain 100% of the legal reserve. The cash reserve requirements to be an A-rated insurance company are very high and much higher than what is required of banks. Your money in a bank's savings account has potentially more risk than that of an insurance company. The FDIC insures your money at the bank up to $250,000. Anything beyond that amount would be at risk if the bank failed.

Insurance companies, on the other hand, have layers of protection. In addition to the high cash reserves and strict regulations, they are required to buy insurance on themselves (re-insurance) from other insurance companies should they have a problem. In addition, the states require insurance companies to pay into a state guaranty fund, which serves as a third layer of protection in the event an insurer becomes insolvent. All 50 states, including Puerto Rico and Washington D.C. maintain a state guaranty fund. The guaranteed limits vary by state, but the most common limits are between **$250,000–$300,000** and can be as much as **$500,000** for both annuities and life insurance, depending upon your state of residence.

Moreover, insurance companies are generally considered safe because they are rated by independent agencies such as A.M. Best, Moody's, Standard & Poor's (S&P), and Fitch. These agencies evaluate the financial strength and creditworthiness of insurers, providing policyholders, investors, and regulators with an assessment of the company's ability to meet its obligations, such as paying out claims.

An Excellent Alternative to Long Term Care Insurance

In Chapter 6 we learned about the risks and costs of long-term care and how your retirement nest egg could be wiped out by a long-term care event. Traditional long-term care insurance has become increasingly difficult to qualify for if you have certain health issues, especially if you have any family history of dementia or Alzheimer's. It is expensive and it's not all that fun to pay for something year after year that you hope you never have to use. Another new and innovative feature of an FIUL is the insurance benefit itself.

Normally, the death benefit is paid out as a tax-free lump sum to your family, but now the death benefit also doubles as long-term care protection while the insured is living. If the insured person is unable to perform two of the six daily living activities (eating, bathing, dressing, toileting, transferring, walking and continence) or a cognitive diagnosis like dementia or Alzheimer's disease, the death benefit can be accessed for the purpose of paying for long-term care.

Life insurance underwriting is based on life expectancy averages, which may be easier to qualify for than traditional long-term care insurance. The death benefit is paid to the insured while living, typically 2% per month over 48 months. For example, with a $500,000 death benefit, 2% of $500,000 = $10,000 every month for 48 months and with no receipts required. With traditional long-term insurance you must pay for the expenses out of pocket and then submit receipts for reimbursement.

With a FIUL policy, if you end up not needing long-term care, then your family will still be receiving a death benefit. It's not a use it or lose it deal like traditional long-term care insurance, which makes this approach much more desirable.

The Costs of an FIUL

What about the costs of a FIUL? Aren't they expensive? Well, that depends upon what you're comparing them to. The costs of these policies are commonly misunderstood. If we are talking about a PROPERLY designed policy for a retirement time horizon of 10 years or more, then the answer is no; they are not expensive. The costs within the early years of a policy are at their highest when the insurance company has the most at risk. But, over time the costs decline substantially. The total accumulative costs and the outcomes are what really matter. Those that say a FIUL/LIRP strategy is too expensive do not understand how they work and are not looking at the full long-term strategy nor the beneficial outcomes achieved. Market based investments start out low and grow over time. On the other hand, life insurance costs start out higher and get lower over time. Like cheese and fine wine, FIUL policies get better as they age assuming they are properly configured and part of a well thought out plan. Again, this is a tool like a chainsaw, very effective when used with skill and caution but dangerous when used inappropriately.

Multiple Benefits of a FIUL

With all factors considered, a properly designed and customized FIUL policy can provide tremendous value. It can help you get to the zero percent tax bracket in retirement, protect you from increasing taxes, and avoid Social Security tax. It can reduce your exposure to market risks, while earning true compound interest. It can also be used as a volatility buffer to protect your "red money" investments against negative sequence risk. It can provide affordable long-term care protection. Most significantly, it can provide a stream of tax-free income in retirement when you need it most, and it can provide a better legacy with an ultimate tax-free payout to your family.

Summary:

- Do not underestimate 21st Century innovation.
- It's nice to have some guarantees.
- Understand the history and evolution of annuities.
- Types of annuities: fixed, variable, and fixed index.
- Fixed-Index Annuities (FIAs) are a modern-day invention.
- The 30+ year bond bull market has ended.
- FIAs are an excellent alternative to bonds.
- FIAs can create more income for life.
- Many modern annuities provide liquidity and penalty-free withdrawals.
- Annuities with zero fees are now available.
- Red tools cost more than green tools over time.
- Understand the advancements and new policy types of life insurance.

- Life Insurance is a uniquely powerful financial tool.
- Life Insurance provides one of the greatest tax advantages available.
- Fixed-Index Universal Life (FIUL) adds the potential for double-digit gains with zero market risk.
- A Life Insurance Retirement Plan (LIRP) is a type of FIUL that also provides tax-free retirement income.
- Insurance companies have layers of protection and are far safer than banks.
- There are new alternatives to long-term care insurance.
- Understand the costs and multiple benefits of a LIRP.

Chapter 9

Debt, Leverage, and Reverse Mortgages

If you have no debt, or very little debt, you may feel like this chapter will not apply to you, but not so fast. How we use or don't use debt can have a tremendous impact on our retirement income and the sustainability of our nest egg. Holistic retirement income planning would not be holistic if we were to ignore the powerful financial tool known as debt.

In working with many clients over many years, I can tell you that the subject of debt is a very emotional subject. The burden of debt is stressful, is often the cause of tension in relationships, and is the cause of much unhappiness.

When debt is abused and used unwisely, it can cause great financial harm. It happens all the time. It is no wonder many people believe all debt is bad and should be shunned like the plague. Is there really such a thing as good debt? I'm here to tell you, when debt is used with skill and good judgement, it can increase our wealth and prosperity and even lower our risks.

Debt can be categorized into two different types: oppressive debt and leverage.

Oppressive debt is "bad" debt and includes credit card debt, payday loans, and other high interest consumer debt. Unfortunately, many people in our country get caught in the trap of living beyond their means and end up carrying debt balances year after year. They struggle to get ahead financially. Debt obligations that can only be satisfied by future earnings are very risky and oppressive in nature and should be avoided. Consumer debt is a common roadblock to prosperity.

Automatic Discipline for Building Wealth and Reducing Debt

Many years ago, my team and I created a unique system for helping clients who were carrying too much oppressive debt. The system uses the power of automation, which is one of the secrets of building wealth. The large majority of folks that are successful in achieving a sizable retirement nest egg have done so as a direct result of having implemented an automatic savings strategy. When I say "automation," I'm referring to automatically saving and/or contributing to an employer retirement plan or investment accounts. After the automatic savings and contributions are set up according to your specific goals, you can essentially forget about it. The contributions will then continue to happen automatically each payday. The comparison between those who use automation and those who don't is like day and night.

Those with oppressive debt can and should use automation as well to help them pay down their debt efficiently and systematically. We are passionate about eliminating bad debt! Not only because of the interest costs, but also because of the huge lost opportunity costs which are a direct result of bad debt. Because debt is such a huge roadblock for so many, I am including the magical debt elimination formula here.

The debt avalanche method focuses on paying off debts by prioritizing those with the highest interest rates first. Here's how it works:

1. **List Debts:** Make a list of all your debts, including their outstanding balances and interest rates.
2. **Order Debts:** Arrange your debts in order from the highest to the lowest interest rate.
3. **Minimum Payments:** Continue making minimum payments on all debts.
4. **Extra Payments:** Allocate any extra funds towards paying off the debt with the highest interest rate.
5. **Compounding Effect:** Once the highest interest debt is paid off, take the money you were putting towards it (including the minimum payment) and apply it to the debt with the next highest interest rate. This creates a "compounding effect" where your total monthly budget remains the same, but your payments going to each debt increase as each debt is paid off. Following this method will significantly accelerate your debt payoff and save yourself a ton of unnecessary interest payments.

The debt snowball method is very similar, but rather than listing the debts by interest rate, you list the debts with the smallest balance first, regardless of interest rates. The debt avalanche method is mathematically optimal. The debt snowball method provides psychological motivation by giving you quick victories as you pay off smaller debts first, which can help you stay motivated to continue paying off debt.

Either method will reduce debt effectively, and both methods require discipline and consistency. This is where automation can make all the difference. Using an automatic bill pay system and then adjusting after each debt is paid off is very effective.

Leverage Can Increase Wealth and Income

Leverage is debt that is used strategically and appropriately to increase wealth. The majority of all strong companies in the world carry some level of debt by choice. The highly paid CFOs of these companies know that credit lines provide greater liquidity and that debt, when used properly, can help their companies grow, allow them to pay less in taxes, and become more profitable as a result. They don't want too much debt, but they also don't want too little.

Some well-known advisors assume that all individuals are too irresponsible and lack the sophistication and the discipline to use leverage to increase personal wealth the way companies and banks do, and therefore consider all debt to be bad debt. I respectfully disagree.

As I have said before, you don't necessarily need to use all the financial tools in the toolbox, including debt. You do, however, need the right combination of tools and strategies to strengthen and optimize your unique financial position and retirement income plan, which may include this tool. Some people will have no need for debt of any kind, but using leverage strategically can make a surprising and welcome improvement for many retirees or soon-to-be retirees.

Paying Cash or Financing

You should understand that the total cost of owning your house is the same whether you finance it or pay cash. Really? Yes really. To illustrate, let's take a look at a comparison between the cost of financing and the gains of investing over a 30- year term assuming the exact same rate.

For example, let's assume we want to buy a new house. Let's also assume that we have $300,000 in the bank and we are trying to decide if we should pay cash in full or finance the house. To keep the math simple, let's assume a $300,000 mortgage with an interest rate of 5%. The monthly payment would be $1,610 and the total interest over the 30-year term = $279,767. Yikes! $279,767 is a lot of interest. Why would anyone choose to pay that if they didn't have to?

Loan Amount	Loan Rate	No. of Years	Monthly Payment	Total Interest Paid	Opportunity Costs of Mortgage Payments
$300,000	5.0%	30	$1,610	$279,767	$1,340,323

What most people think about and stress over is the interest on the loan. However, the larger cost is the lost opportunity costs of $1,340,323. Regardless of what we may think, if the house is paid for with cash in one lump sum, or financed for 30 years, the lost opportunity costs come out the exact same.

Lump Sum Invested	Rate of Return	No. of Years	Monthly Payment	Total Interest Earned	Investment Account Balance
$300,000	5.0%	30	0	$1,040,323	$1,340,323

The same is true if, instead of investing a lump sum, we invest the monthly amount of $1,610 for 30 years, the total investment would grow to the same $1,340,323.

Lump Sum Invested	Rate of Return	No. of Years	Monthly Investment	Total Interest Earned	Investment Account Balance
0	5.0%	30	$1,610	$1,040,323	$1,340,323

Understanding this concept, we can better consider all possible opportunities available to us.

Equity Earns 0%

When your money goes into a house it changes form and becomes equity. You no longer have liquidity, or use, of that money. Equity in your home earns a zero percent rate of return. Do not confuse appreciating property values and equity. Property values will appreciate or depreciate regardless of whether the property has a mortgage or not.

Keeping Your Money Employed

I believe everyone should seek to have their house completely paid for as fast as possible. My team and I have helped many of our clients to accomplish this goal. However, having your house paid for does not necessarily have to mean that you don't choose to use a mortgage to achieve leverage.

Banks and large companies know how to leverage other people's money (OPM) to make money, and homeowners may be able to do so as well.

Our money will work for us by earning us more money if we allow it to do its job. Even though it may sound like a great thing to pay off a mortgage or pay cash for a house instead of financing it, we are laying off our workforce when we take this route. When we put money into a house it transforms into equity. Equity is lazy, and it just sits there in the walls of your home doing nothing. Let's explore the idea of investing our money, rather than paying off a mortgage early.

In the illustrations above, we used a 5% loan rate and a 5% investment return, and the ultimate outcome was the exact same. However, even in that scenario, there can be some benefits for using a mortgage and putting less money into the house. The main benefits are not derived from possible tax deductions, but rather from inflation protection, and much greater liquidity, use, and control of your money.

A Hedge Against Inflation

When you consider the effects of inflation, the dollars we have today are our most valuable. Inflation is a major consideration in paying down a mortgage. Remember, inflation has averaged 3.24% over the past 100 years, and 4.08% over the past 50 years. A 30-year mortgage with a locked in fixed-rate can help you hedge against inflation.

If you have a mortgage payment today of $1,610 and we assume an inflation rate of 3%, in 10 years that $1,610 payment is going to feel like $1,197. In 20 years, it's going to feel like $891, and $663 in 30 years.

As you can see, you may benefit by not prepaying your mortgage with inflated dollars and keep your money invested with the opportunity to perhaps keep up with or get ahead of inflation.

Maintaining Liquidity, Use, and Control

Equity in your home is typically not liquid and could become inaccessible. Your circumstances and the changing economy may prevent you from accessing cash from your house when you need it the most.

In order to access the equity in your home, you typically need to sell the home or to demonstrate to the bank that you can qualify for an equity loan or cash out refinance, which may become a problem for you down the road.

Maintaining liquidity, use, and control of your money is one of the major reasons for considering using leverage. If you keep your extra money out of the house, and instead put it in a side account, assuming that you can grow the money at a rate at least equal to the interest rate on your loan, then you have greater flexibility and control.

If you have enough money to pay off your mortgage at any time, do you really have debt? Technically yes, but it may be "good debt," or leverage if it's working to your advantage. Proper use of leverage may increase your wealth and reduce many other risks, not the other way around.

Earning a Spread

We can potentially earn more return with our money than it costs us to borrow. In the example above, we assumed a 5% fixed rate loan and a 5% investment return. What if you could do better than that? If you have a 4% mortgage and you can achieve a 6% return, there is a clear financial advantage. This is called earning a spread. This is what the banks do all of the time with your money. You may be in a position to earn a spread on their money via a mortgage.

Loan Amount	Loan Rate	No. of Years	Monthly Payment	Total Interest Paid	Opportunity Costs of Mortgage Payments
$300,000	4.0%	30	$1,432	$215,609	$994,049

Lump Sum Invested	Rate of Return	No. of Years	Monthly Payment	Total Interest Paid	Investment Account Balance
$300,000	6.0%	30	0	$1,506,773	$1,806,773

What About the Risk?

At this point, critics will point out that there are risks associated with investing and no guarantees on rates of return. They may say you should not put your home at risk, and in many cases I would agree. However, it very much depends upon your unique financial situation.

When it comes to homes and mortgages, many people are understandably uncomfortable assuming the risks associated with investments. Nowadays, however, as discussed in previous chapters, there are powerful green financial tools available that provide market-like returns with indexing strategies, but with no downside market risk. This is truly revolutionary.

Leverage Can Reduce Risk

When used correctly, leverage does not put a home at risk and even lowers many of the risks faced in retirement. If you had the liquid assets available in the example above, you could simply pay off the mortgage at any given moment in time if you wanted to. If your wealth is increasing though, you would likely not be in a hurry to stop the compounding growth. It's a question of "do I keep my money working for me or do I put it to sleep within the walls of my home?"

The Paid Off Mortgage Dream

Many people have spent years and years working toward the goal of paying off their mortgage. Regardless of the math, the lost opportunity costs, and the other benefits, they mentally want the mortgage paid off. If that is you, I completely understand and that's perfectly okay. The goal here is to make sure you are aware of your options to potentially increase your wealth, stability, and financial peace of mind. If paying off the mortgage gives you peace of mind, then by all means do it. However, if you have a paid off house, but lack sufficient retirement income, (house rich and cash poor) that may not bring the financial peace you had hoped for.

Other Scenarios

The example above was based on the question, "should we pay cash for a house or finance and invest the money instead?" The example assumes you have enough liquid assets to pay cash for a house, but let's consider other common scenarios based on what we have learned.

1. Will making extra principal payments save you money?
2. Is a 15-year term mortgage better than a 30-year mortgage?
3. On a new purchase, is a large down payment better than a small down payment?

If our goal is to use leverage and keep our money working for us, then we would want the mortgage term to be as long as possible. We would not be interested in putting more money into the house than necessary in the form of extra principal payments or a large down payment on a new purchase. I realize it may be a challenge to get your mind wrapped around this concept. It helps if you try to think more from a banker's perspective rather than with a consumer's perspective.

What if you are in retirement or approaching retirement and your mortgage is already paid off or if only a fairly small balance remains?

The HECM Reverse Mortgage

If you have sufficient assets and tax efficient income and no concerns about running out of money in retirement, then you may not need to do anything with the equity in your house. It can just sit there inside the walls until you and/or your spouse complete your life's journey. After death, your heirs will likely sell the house and liquidate the equity. It depends upon what is most important to you: leaving the full value of the house for an inheritance or enjoying more income in retirement. This leads us to the subject of the Home Equity Conversion Mortgage (HECM) aka reverse mortgage.

The first known reverse mortgage was created in 1961 by Nelson Haynes of Deering Savings & Loan. It was created for the widow of a high school football coach in Portland, Maine. This was done as an act of kindness to help her stay in her home after her husband's death. The idea had appeal and started to spread. In 1988, President Ronald Reagan signed the Housing and Community Development Act, which enabled federal insurance for reverse mortgages. In 1989, Marjorie Mason of Fairway, Kansas was the first recipient of an FHA-insured Home Equity Conversion Mortgage (HECM).

In the years that followed, the reverse mortgage has gone through many changes and improvements and has evolved into a unique and useful financial tool. The early versions of the HECM are nothing like what is available today. The Reverse Mortgage Stabilization Act of 2013 resolved many of the negative issues of the past and now homeowners always remain on the title of the home.

The HECM reverse mortgage allows homeowners to convert a portion of their home's equity into tax-free money and they never need to worry about making loan payments. The strategic use of an HECM can lower many of the other risks you face in retirement.

There are a variety of ways to strategically use and benefit from a HECM reverse mortgage, including purchasing a new home with a HECM, refinancing an existing mortgage into an HECM, or establishing a credit line that allows the homeowners to access the equity when needed. The proceeds can be taken as a lump sum, as a line of credit, or as regular monthly tax-free payments, as long as you live (tenure) or for a specific term. The HECM provides flexibility and the ability to adjust based on your needs.

A Reverse Mortgage Can Protect Your Investment Portfolio

Access to home equity can be a cushion for emergencies, and it can also be used as a volatility buffer to protect your investment portfolio against a negative sequence of returns, as discussed in Chapter 4. For example, rather than pulling income from an investment-based portfolio during a bear market, you could pull tax-free money from your home equity. This one strategy alone can make a very big difference in retirement outcomes and investment portfolio sustainability.

Multiple Strategic Ways to Use a HECM.

1. Make your monthly mortgage payment optional rather than required.
2. Establish a permanent guaranteed line of credit (that grows).
3. Use the tax-free funds to pay the taxes on a Roth conversion plan to enable a tax-free retirement.
4. Help cover health insurance during early retirement prior to Medicare eligibility at age 65.
5. Use line of credit to delay and maximize Social Security benefits until age 70.
6. Help pay for long-term health care needs.
7. Use as a volatility buffer to protect against market and sequence risk.
8. Use to convert a room or basement to a living facility for an aging parent or caregiver.

Combine proceeds with the sale of your current home to buy a new home without monthly mortgage payments.

Children's Inheritance

What about the inheritance for the kids? Most people hope to leave a legacy, if possible, but most are not willing to struggle financially through retirement for the sole purpose of passing on more assets to the kids. If you need to use a portion of your home equity to improve and stabilize your retirement, then once you and/or your spouse are gone, the kids will still inherit the remaining equity in the house along with any other assets you may have. The house will be sold, and any mortgage balance will be paid off, and your heirs will receive the remaining equity. Your children would also have the option of paying off the mortgage and keeping the home, if desired.

A Wonderful Contract

Robert C. Merton, Distinguished Professor of Finance, MIT Sloan School & Nobel Laureate – Economics 1997, is a strong advocate of using housing wealth to solve the global longevity challenge. He said, "A reverse mortgage is both a stream of income as a hedge and an asset. It changes from the former to the latter when the people in the house no longer need it. The reverse mortgage recognizes it by saying, 'As long as you're in the house, you pay nothing, even if you live to be 120.' When you're not there, your heirs get the unspent cash from the reverse mortgage and they can sell the house, pay the amount due, keep the difference, or let the bank take the house if the amount owed exceeds the value of the house. That's a wonderful contract!"

A HECM reverse mortgage is a financial tool that you may or may not need. For those who have a smaller retirement nest egg but substantial equity in their home, it can be especially beneficial. Even more beneficial if mortgage payments are still being made.

There have been many case studies done regarding the use of tapping into housing wealth in retirement and the outcomes are very compelling. When using Monte Carlo simulations, the probability of success (not running out of money) improves from 58% to 96%! As a financial advisor who provides holistic retirement income planning, I cannot ignore this tool because of the positive way it can impact a client's retirement outcomes.

Qualifying for a HECM

Qualifying for a HECM can be easier than qualifying for a traditional mortgage. You will likely qualify if you are over age 62 and you have a fair amount of equity in your home. Typically, you will need at least 60% equity or more. There is also a financial assessment to verify your ability to pay for the non-mortgage expenses of owning a home, including property taxes, home maintenance and upkeep, homeowner's insurance, and other required property expenses, such as HOA dues, condo dues, etc.

If you are making mortgage payments, you could use an HECM to simply end all future mortgage payments! You may **not** need to worry about getting that remaining balance paid off if you don't want to. A HECM line of credit can give you guaranteed access to a portion of the equity in your home, regardless of market conditions or tightening credit. A HECM may be worth considering if for no other reason than having an emergency buffer. The HECM is one method to unlock the wealth stored inside the walls of your home.

Using a HECM to Maximize Social Security

Social Security provides an incentive to delay starting your benefits. Each year you delay claiming your benefits, beyond your full retirement age, you earn "delayed retirement credits" of 8%. You can do this each year until age 70. For example, if income from a HECM allows you to delay claiming Social Security until age 70, and assuming an FRA (Full Retirement Age) of 66, this would make your Social Security 32% larger for the rest of your life and/or spouses life. This could easily translate into $300,000 or $400,000 of additional accumulative Social Security income depending upon longevity. The HECM can provide a way for many to bridge the gap and increase their retirement income.

Summary

- Oppressive debt causes financial harm.
- A key to success for building wealth and reducing debt is using the debt avalanche or debt snowball method and automating the process.
- Using debt or leverage wisely can increase wealth and income.
- Paying cash for a house has the same ultimate costs as financing with a mortgage.
- Keeping your money employed is a good idea.

- Proper use of leverage can reduce risk.
- You may want to reconsider the paid-off mortgage idea.
- Maintaining liquidity, use, and control of your money has advantages.
- Equity always earns a 0% rate of return.
- New and improved reverse mortgages can protect your investment portfolio.
- A HECM reverse mortgage can help you increase your Social Security benefit.

Chapter 10

Advisor Alpha and Advisor Gamma

Quantifying the Value of a Good Advisor

Vanguard academics set out to quantify the added value of using a financial advisor. They completed the well-known "Advisor's Alpha" study in 2001. The research documents that a good financial advisor can add a 3% return on average (above beta) to a client's investment portfolio annually. It is a good study and it's nice to see that the value of an advisor can be quantified. However, the Advisor's Alpha study is only considering the performance of a "traditional asset allocation" investment portfolio. The value and synergy that can be created with holistic planning is not at all represented.

The academic research team at Morningstar recognized that alpha and beta are only two elements of a myriad of important financial planning decisions. There are many other planning elements that can have a far more significant impact on retirement income.

"Alpha, Beta, and Now... Gamma" Study

Morningstar research academics took on the task of quantifying the value of holistic retirement income planning. The "Alpha, Beta, and Now... Gamma" study was published in 2013 and was able to document the data and quantify a 22.6% increase in retirement income over the "traditional asset allocation" 3% alpha approach. That's a big deal! Truly "the whole is greater than the sum of its parts." Increasing your retirement income by 22.6% by simply obtaining better holistic planning will be welcome news to many people approaching retirement.

As revealing and important as this study is, it too is limited in scope. The study only included five of the many different financial planning decisions/techniques that should be considered. The researchers acknowledge this fact within the study saying, "There are definitely other decisions that can be as, if not more, important than the five reviewed."

The five categories included in the Morningstar study:

1. Total wealth framework (including Social Security)
2. Withdrawal strategy
3. Incorporating guaranteed income products (i.e., annuities)
4. Tax-efficient decisions
5. Liability-relative asset allocation optimization.

Not only was the study limited to these five categories, but the techniques within each category were also limited in scope. For example, the "tax-efficient decisions" used in the study included the types of investments best located in the taxable bucket, tax deferred bucket, and the best order of withdrawal. But it did not consider Roth accounts or Roth Conversions, which can have a tremendous impact in protecting against higher taxes in the future. When all available techniques are used to optimize a retirement plan, the added value is often much greater than 22.6%. Every individual situation is unique and will vary. However, when we talk about cumulative, long-term income, the added value and impact of good holistic planning can increase your retirement income by double or triple the 22.6%. Double or triple is not an exaggeration. Reducing lifetime taxes by 50% or more will increase the percentage of gamma considerably. Understandably, there are so many variables, it is difficult to include every technique/decision in one generalized study.

In the game of chess, each player has 16 pieces, which includes one king, one queen, two rooks, two bishops, two knights, and eight pawns. The chessboard has a total of 64 squares. How many possible chess positions do you think are possible? If you guessed billions or trillions, you are way low. The number is quattuordecillion, an extremely large number with 45 zeros... 1,000,000,000,000,000,000 ,000,000,000,000,000,000,000,000,000.

Our Financial Life Has Many Variables

The number of variables and possible decisions in holistic retirement planning is also a much larger number than commonly thought. One example would be the number of variables associated with claiming Social Security benefits. By itself, there are more than 500 claiming decision variables. When we consider strategies to avoid Social Security taxation, as well as the optimization of other assets and income, the number of variables is large.

We are nearing the end of this book. If your perspective on the value of holistic planning has changed, then the purpose of this book has been achieved. The concepts and information presented here, when properly applied, can protect and grow your wealth and substantially improve your retirement outlook.

Conflicting Opinions and Outdated Practices

Within the financial services industry, we find a mixture of conflicting opinions and outdated practices. How is a person to know who is best qualified to assist them with something as important as your retirement nest egg and the future income you and your family will depend on over many years in the future?

I have rubbed shoulders with many financial advisors of all types over the years and I can say most all that I know are hardworking men and woman of integrity. These are good people who want to do what is right and what is in the best interest of their clients.

However, their employers, or the system in which they work, controls and limits what they can and cannot do, and that is a problem.

So, what's the next step? How do you obtain quality holistic retirement planning? How do you find the right kind of advisor with the skills and experience necessary to help you optimize and map out the chess pieces that make up your retirement plan?

Finding the right kind of advisor can be a very difficult task. How do you know who to trust to help you create a truly holistic retirement plan? In the appendix, I provide ten key points to assist you in identifying the right kind of advisor.

Time is of the essence and the sooner you get started the better. Do not be discouraged if you are getting a late start. Even if you are already retired, your existing plan and investments can likely be improved and optimized.

A Retirement Blueprint

Let me share with you a quick story that I remember hearing from a railroad worker many years ago by the name of Gordon B. Hinckley. He said that one day he received a telephone call from his counterpart in Newark, New Jersey, who said that a passenger train had arrived without its baggage car. The patrons were angry.

They discovered that the train had been properly prepared up in Oakland, California, and properly delivered to St. Louis, from which station it was to be carried to its destination on the east coast. But, in the St. Louis yards, a thoughtless switch operator had moved a piece of steel just three inches.

That piece of steel was a switch point, and the car that should have been in Newark, New Jersey, was in New Orleans, Louisiana, thirteen hundred miles away.

This story demonstrates how small decisions, or the lack there of, even those that appear insignificant at the time, can lead to unexpected and sometimes profound consequences—Consequences that can result in frustration and possibly unrealized dreams. This principle holds true with any journey, especially a long journey like retirement which spans two or three decades. You need to know where you are going and how you are going to get there. Surprisingly, fewer than 20% of retirees have a written retirement blueprint.

A Monte Carlo simulation illustrating the odds of success is not a written plan. A stack of financial statements is not a written plan. A written plan encompasses documentation for an income strategy, integrates and optimizes Social Security benefits, ensures liquidity for emergencies, and outlines a year-by-year roadmap for Roth conversions and other tax strategies. It also includes provisions to mitigate inflation and manage investment volatility effectively. Additionally, it addresses healthcare and long-term care needs, alongside a comprehensive legacy plan. Such a detailed plan provides the clarity and structure necessary to navigate the complexities of financial planning with confidence and foresight.

The 5Ws represent the five critical areas of wealth management. To create efficiencies and optimize your wealth, it is essential to holistically coordinate each of these areas.

They include:

1. Income Planning
2. Investment Planning
3. Tax Planning
4. Health Care Planning
5. Legacy/Estate Planning

The 5W planning process looks like this.

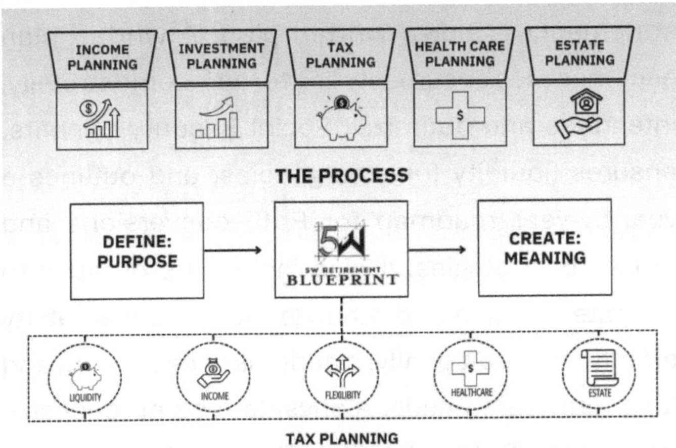

The 5W RETIREMENT BLUEPRINT financial planning services are focused on five critical pieces of the retirement planning puzzle to help our clients achieve their optimal retirement.

Estate Planning

Estate planning is perhaps the most procrastinated aspect of financial planning. It's one of those tasks you know you need to tackle (or update), yet it often fails to become a top priority. Initially, it feels complex and expensive, and there's always a myriad of other activities you'd prefer to spend your time on.

By crafting a comprehensive estate plan, you ensure that your assets are distributed according to your wishes, minimizing potential conflicts and ensuring financial security for your loved ones. Without a plan in place, the distribution of your estate may fall under state probate laws, which could result in unintended consequences and unnecessary taxes. The probate process is often slow, taking a year or more, and can be both tedious and stressful for the family. Estate planning is much more than probate avoidance. It includes specific healthcare directives in case of incapacity and can potentially reduce estate taxes through strategic planning. Delaying estate planning only increases the risk of leaving your loved ones unprepared and vulnerable to legal and financial challenges during an already difficult time.

When you bite the bullet and just decide to get it taken care of, you will most likely be surprised that it was easier than you had imagined and even less expensive than anticipated.

Summary

- Understanding and quantifying the value of a good advisor.
- Morningstar's "Alpha, Beta, and Now... Gamma" study confirms a 22.6% advantage.

- Our financial lives have many variables.
- Holistic planning provides great value.
- Beware of outdated practices, conflicting opinions, and bias.
- Don't procrastinate estate planning.

Appendix

Finding a 21st Century Holistic Retirement Income Planner/Advisor

The following ten points can assist you in your search for the right kind of advisor:

1. Is the advisor a fiduciary with complete transparency?

There are two standards within the financial services industry that are important for you to understand: The Suitability Standard and the Fiduciary Standard.

The Fiduciary Standard is the highest standard and requires an independent fiduciary advisor to place his or her own interests below that of the client's interests. In other words, a fiduciary advisor has a legal responsibility to be transparent and always act in the best interest of his or her client. You would assume that is always the case, but the industry, from its roots, was built on the much lower "suitability" standard, which is opaque in nature and still dominates the industry today. When operating under the suitability standard, it doesn't matter who benefits more, the client or advisor, as long as an investment is considered to be "suitable."

The big box broker/dealers and their registered representatives are in the business of selling "suitable" financial products. Brokers, by definition, are in the business of brokering or selling, NOT planning.

Only a relatively small percentage of financial advisors in the United States adhere to the Fiduciary Standard; it is a small but growing number. The broker/dealer world is large and powerful, but as people gain a better understanding of how things work within the industry, I believe the industry will ultimately be forced to change. The current financial incentives deter many, but more and more advisors are resigning from their big box firms and surrendering their broker status.

Advisors who make the transition from broker to independent investment advisor are required to change the way they are compensated. Most are not too excited about taking a pay cut, which explains why the majority hang onto the suitability standard. Making the transition also requires the advisor to assume the responsibilities that come with being a legal fiduciary, which includes more responsibility, which is not very appealing.

Transparency is a requirement of a fiduciary and includes disclosing any possible conflicts of interest. Independent investment advisors are paid for providing financial advice, not for selling. **Brokers work for their firm, but fiduciaries work for the client.**

Aligning yourself with an independent fiduciary should be a top priority and non-negotiable. Why would anyone choose to use an advisor or firm that is unwilling or unable to commit to the Fiduciary Standard? This is your life savings we are talking about, so why not demand transparency?

Now, the Fiduciary Standard is important, but it is not enough. All fiduciaries are not equal. Just because someone is a fiduciary advisor does not mean they are a skilled holistic income planner. Some fiduciary firms are "red tools only" firms and they have a strong bias against green financial tools, viewing them as competition to what they do. This is common when a well-established brokerage firm makes the transition from the suitability to Fiduciary Standard. Yes, they have become transparent and changed their fee structure, but they are still steeped in "traditional asset allocation" and are still using outdated strategies.

Is it possible for an advisor to truly do what is in the best interest of their client if they arbitrarily exclude many of the financial tools available? Absolutely not! Each tool, with its unique attributes, should be available without bias to create the most optimal financial plan possible. By limiting themselves and their clients to "red tools only" (mutual funds, stocks, and bonds) and excluding green tools with guarantees (fixed index annuities and fixed index life insurance), I would argue that they are not living up to their fiduciary responsibility to do what is in the best interest of the client.

If an advisor or firm hold themselves out as investment advisors only, and do not attempt to provide retirement income planning, then that would be legitimate. In this case, their clients would recognize the limited scope of their investment services. If a firm labels themselves as retirement income planners, and they are working with only half a toolbox, then I would avoid that firm. This would clue you in that they are biased and not true holistic retirement income planners.

2. Does the advisor have a complete financial toolbox?

If the advisor is a "red financial tools only" advisor, or a "green financial tools only" advisor, they will have a strong bias. The advice will be limited to one way of thinking, rather than utilizing the right combination of unique financial attributes and strengths of all tools available. The best holistic plans often use a combination.

3. Does the advisor specialize in holistic retirement planning?

It is common for financial advisors to do some degree of planning, but most of them operate within a limited scope. In such situations, the financial efficiencies we are looking for (Gamma) will be less than they would be when working with a true holistic planner.

4. Does the advisor use mutual funds?

If an advisor uses mutual funds, this is an easy way to identify that they are not current with the times. There is no reason to continue to use underperforming mutual funds with all their inefficiencies in a retirement income plan. If you are pre-retirement and still contributing into an employer plan, such as a 401k, then your investment options will be limited and will likely include mutual funds. Taking advantage of a company match, if one is offered, is very valuable. Take the free money but contributing over and above the match is not advisable. There are better ways to invest outside of an employer plan if you are contributing above the match.

5. Is the advisor independent or affiliated with a broker/dealer?

Brokers/dealers have tight control over their registered representatives and limit the tools within their advisor's toolbox. Their product offerings are pre-engineered to benefit the brokerage firm.

6. Does your advisor/firm offer any proprietary funds?

For business owners, having something proprietary is usually a good thing. But for consumers, the opposite is true regarding investment products. Many firms create their own proprietary products/ funds and advise clients to include them in their portfolio. Advisors are incentivized to use in-house proprietary funds. This is a conflict of interest if there ever was one and allows the firm to charge you twice. Broker/ dealers can get away with this, but not fiduciaries. Make sure your advisor/firm does not offer any proprietary funds.

7. Is a bigger firm better than a smaller, independent firm?

When uncertain about who to trust, consumers tend to gravitate to big box firms because of name recognition. If a firm is large, it must be a good choice, right? I review and analyze portfolios from big box firms on a regular basis when new prospective clients bring in their statements, and I can assure you that bigger is not better. Big box firms are fat and sluggish. Envision the Titanic, a big fancy ship. They could see a problem on the horizon (an iceberg). They tried to turn and slow down the ship, but the ship was too big, and they were unable to avoid the disaster. On the other hand, if you were in a smaller private yacht traveling alongside the Titanic, the captain could easily navigate around the iceberg. Independent firms have all options on the table. Big box firms have only their options on the table and most of them are trapped in the mutual fund world.

8. Is the advisory firm also the custodian?

Big box brokers typically act as their own custodian of funds. This is how Bernie Madoff "made off" with billions of his clients' dollars. You should never give money directly to an advisor's firm. Independent investment advisors will not accept or take personal custody of funds, and they will always use third-party custodial banks. Your rollovers and transfers should always be direct trustee-to-trustee transfers where they are tightly regulated and it's easy to follow the money with 24/7 online access to transaction history and monthly statements sent to you directly from the independent institution. As previously mentioned, most advisors I have had the pleasure of associating with over the years have impeccably high integrity.

It is unfortunate that a few bad apples can spoil the apple cart. Nowadays, an advisor is often assumed to be guilty until proven innocent.

9. Does the advisor ever sell variable annuities or variable life insurance?

I don't like to label any financial tool as either all good or all bad because it has more to do with when and how to use certain tools or when not to use them. However, I would be very wary of anyone recommending variable annuities or variable life because far better tools exist today. You will want to work with someone with a good understanding of the newer fixed index products.

10. Can the advisor create "Gamma"?

It is important to consider if the advisor possesses the skills and specialization of holistic income planning. This is the hardest type of advisor to find because there are not nearly as many of them available. You will not find them in the large well known national firms, those firms are usually rooted in tradition and are typically all red or all green and only give lip service to holistic planning. Traditional planning ignores many of the elements that can create efficiencies. In the past, we attempted to maintain a national list of qualified financial advisors who have embraced the Fiduciary Standard and who specialize in holistic retirement planning, and we did this as a resource for providing referrals. However, with the advances in technology and the ease of meeting with clients remotely nowadays, we have for the most part stopped making referrals. Over the years, I have developed a wonderful team of holistic financial planners with the ability to service clients within the Unted States. We have a very specific planning process we call the 5W Retirement Blueprint.

If you're looking for this type of personalized financial planning, we invite you to consider working with our firm. It's important to ensure we're the right fit for each other, and we're excited to offer a complimentary consultation to discuss your unique needs and explore the possibilities. Let's take the first step together—schedule your consultation today!

To schedule a free consultation, you can contact our office at 480-550-6556 or send an email to Blueprint@MartinsenWealth.com

About the Author

Lane G. Martinsen is the Founder and CEO of Martinsen Wealth Management, LLC, an SEC Registered Investment Advisor. He is a Certified Financial Fiduciary® and a Retirement Income Certified Professional (RICP®).

Lane graduated from the University of Phoenix and completed CFP® Certification Education at the University of Arizona, as well as post undergraduate studies at The American College of Financial Services. He is the host of the popular YouTube channel, Financial Fast Lane. He is also certified in long term care planning CLTC® and Social Security planning NSSA®.

Lane has a diverse background within the financial services industry that began in 1988. In addition to serving his own clients, Lane has trained and mentored a growing team of holistic financial planners, serving clients around the United States.

Lane and his wife Tara met in college while attending Brigham Young University in Idaho. They have 5 children and 11 grandchildren. Lane considers being a husband and father his greatest accomplishments, with a deep love of God, family, and country.

For More Information

https://www.MartinsenWealth.com

Made in United States
Troutdale, OR
06/18/2025

32207613R00130